'For the scientist who is a Christian, the exploration of the natural world is not just the joy of intellectual curiosity but is an act of worship enhancing prayer and the reading of the Bible. In this book we get an insight into that worship which is both inspiring and challenging for our own relationship with Jesus.'
The Revd Professor David Wilkinson, Project Director, Equipping Christian Leadership in an Age of Science, St John's College, Durham University

'This book fills a crucial gap by encouraging us to use all that science tells us about our world and universe to help us to worship and pray in a deeper and more informed way. It will be a great help in engaging with the many major developments of our time, such as climate change and AI, in a more reflective and rounded way. It will appeal to a broad range of church traditions and I hope it will be very widely used in private devotions and corporate worship.'
Bishop Richard Cheetham, Member of the Anglican Communion Science Commission, Fellow of the International Society for Science and Religion

BRF Ministries

15 The Chambers, Vineyard
Abingdon OX14 3FE
+44 (0)1865 319700 | brf.org.uk

Bible Reading Fellowship (BRF) is a charity (233280)
and company limited by guarantee (301324),
registered in England and Wales

EU Authorised Representative: Easy Access System Europe –
Mustamäe tee 50, 10621 Tallinn, Estonia, **gpsr.requests@easproject.com**

ISBN 978 1 80039 285 4
First published 2025
10 9 8 7 6 5 4 3 2 1 0
All rights reserved

Text © Ruth M. Bancewicz and The Faraday Institute for Science and Religion 2025
This edition © Bible Reading Fellowship 2025
Photo credits: see page 158

Scripture quotations marked with the following abbreviations are taken from the version shown. NRSV: the New Revised Standard Version Updated Edition. Copyright © 2021 National Council of Churches of Christ in the United States of America. Used by permission. All rights reserved worldwide. NIV: The Holy Bible, New International Version® Anglicized, NIV® Copyright © 1979, 1984, 2011 by Biblica, Inc.® Used by permission. All rights reserved worldwide. NLT: The Holy Bible, New Living Translation, copyright © 1996, 2004, 2007, 2013. Used by permission of Tyndale House Publishers, Inc., Carol Stream, Illinois 60188. All rights reserved. ESV: The Holy Bible, English Standard Version, published by HarperCollins Publishers, © 2001 Crossway Bibles, a division of Good News Publishers. Used by permission. All rights reserved.

Every effort has been made to trace and contact copyright owners for material used in this resource. We apologise for any inadvertent omissions or errors, and would ask those concerned to contact us so that full acknowledgement can be made in the future.

A catalogue record for this book is available from the British Library

Printed and bound in the UK by Zenith Media NP4 0DQ
Printed on 100% post-consumer recycled paper

The WORKS of the LORD

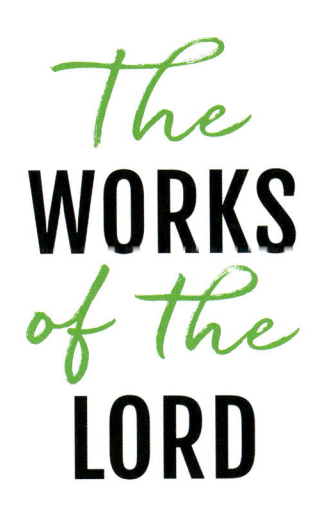

52 biblical reflections on science, technology and creation

EDITED BY
RUTH M. BANCEWICZ

BRF
Ministries

CONTENTS

Introduction 8

Part I The heavens declare

1. God as faithful creator 13
2. God's creatures...........................15
3. God's good creation 17
4. The creative creation 19
5. Discerning wisdom through playful, childlike enjoyment 21
6. Praiseworthy 23
7. Rest 26

Part II Christ and creation

8. New beginnings...........................30
9. Christ the creator 32
10. Evidence and the supremacy of Christ...34
11. Powerful...36
12. Choosing good trees 39

Part III Exploring creation

- **13** Delighting in bountiful creation .. 45
- **14** On the ocean 48
- **15** Transcendence 50
- **16** Ecosystems and biodiversity 52
- **17** Using creation to heal 55
- **18** Through the telescope 58
- **19** In the lab 60
- **20** God, the true master craftsman .. 62
- **21** Through the microscope lens 64

Part IV Being human

- **22** Care for the vulnerable 69
- **23** The image of God 72
- **24** Care for the suffering 74
- **25** The unborn child 77
- **26** Disability and gene editing 80
- **27** End of life 83

Part V More than human?

- **28** Crowned with glory! Guided by AI?....................89
- **29** Embodied 91
- **30** The image of God 93
- **31** AI and gardening 95
- **32** Fallen 97
- **33** Work and rest 99
- **34** Idolatry 102
- **35** Begotten 104
- **36** Manners matter................106
- **37** Creativity 108
- **38** Comforting words 110
- **39** Protectors........................112
- **40** Incarnated teaching........114
- **41** Increasingly human 116

Part VI Caring for creation

42 Till and keep 121
43 Broken relationships 124
44 Broken world 127
45 The earth mourns......................130
46 God's commitment 133
47 Creation is still good 137
48 Sustainer......................139
49 Hope for today 142
50 Hope for the future....................145
51 Release from eco-anxiety 148
52 Freedom to live...........................151

Index of reflections by contributor 155
Acknowledgements 157
Photo credits 158

INTRODUCTION

For a long time I have wanted to have a devotional book to put into people's hands that gently brings together insights from science and Christian faith in a way that is relevant for any reader. I am delighted to be able to do that now, bringing together contributions by 43 scientists and theologians. The writers are mainly from the UK, but also include voices from Romania, Zimbabwe, Sri Lanka, Malaysia, Canada, Peru and Hong Kong.

Most of these devotions were originally written for *New Daylight* or *Guidelines* Bible reading notes, published by BRF Ministries. They have been updated and edited where necessary and arranged into sections – each with a brief introduction. Where the Bible passage is just a few verses, it is included in the text; where it is longer, a selection of key verses is included. You will need to get hold of, or download, a Bible, to look up the full passages. Some of the Bible passages are repeated throughout the book, because each contributor is bringing a unique perspective on what may be a familiar passage.

Our suggestion is to use one devotion each week over a year, maybe on a day when you have a bit more time to read, reflect and pray. They might also be useful as starter for a time of reflection during a science-focused event. Preachers might like to use them as a source of sermon ideas or stories to tell to introduce particular passages from the Bible.

However you use this book, I pray that you find its contents both inspirational and challenging, helping your faith to grow deeper roots into God's word.

Ruth M. Bancewicz, Church Engagement Director, The Faraday Institute for Science and Religion

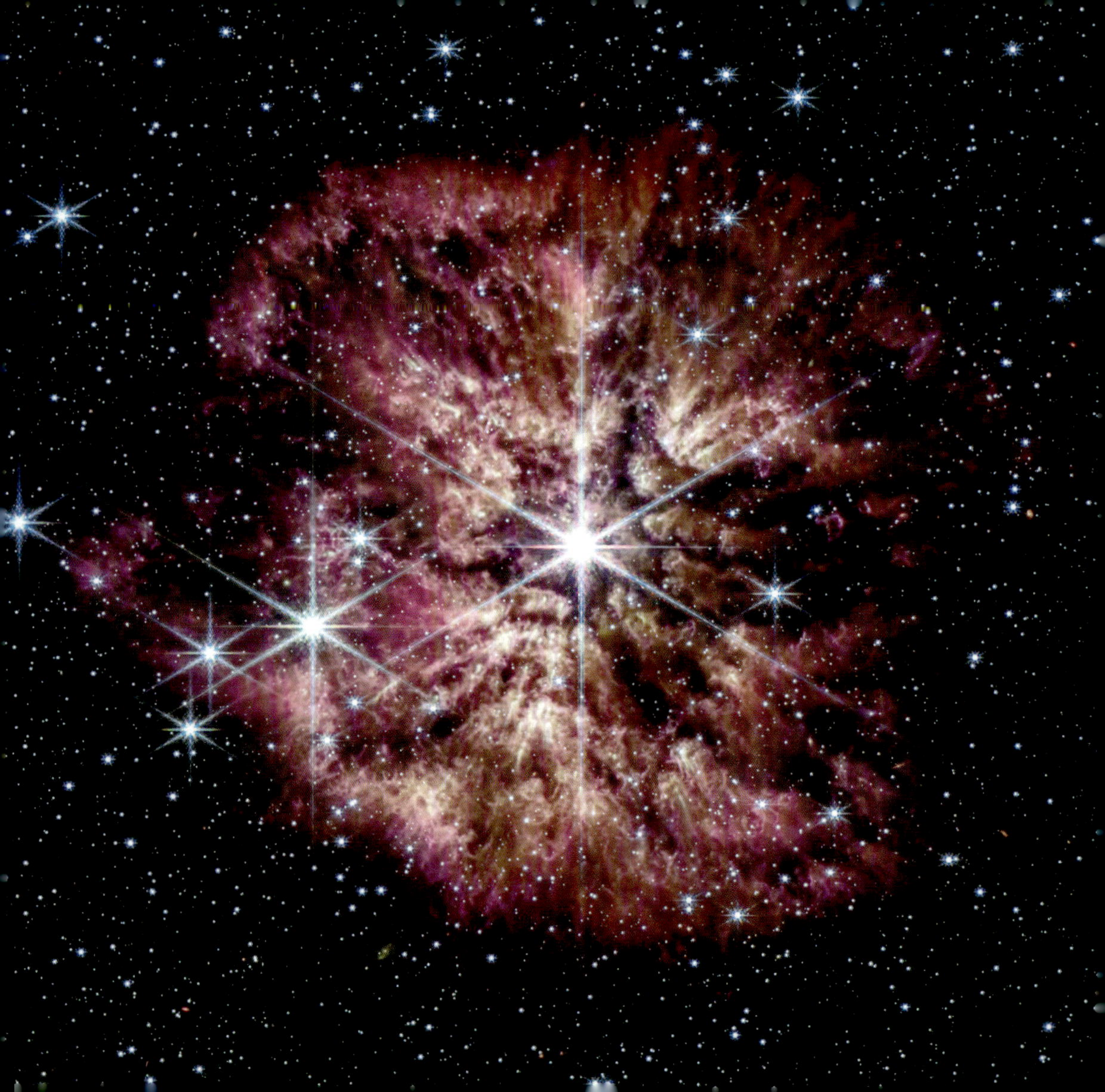

PART I
THE HEAVENS DECLARE

Not many of us are scientists, but we can all enjoy the excitement of learning something new about the world. You might have been fascinated by something you saw on visit to a national park, a new bird appearing in your garden or a nature documentary. Each of us will find that different things provoke our curiosity, prompting us to think of those questions adults often forget to ask: 'What is it?', 'What's it for?' and 'Why?'

We understand far more about the mechanisms of how things came to be than the biblical writers could have imagined. We know about the Big Bang and how living things developed and became more complex over time. We can appreciate the huge diversity and interconnectedness of life on earth. The things we learn about the

Opposite: a Wolf-Rayet star, which is the prelude to a supernova, captured by James Webb space telescope

world widen our perspective, giving us a bigger picture of creation and the creator. That informed perspective can help us praise God all the more: what a wonderful world he made!

Drawing on a variety of creation passages throughout the Old and New Testaments, in this section we will share just a few of the wonders revealed by science, looking at how this perspective expands and enhances our own view of God as creator. I hope you enjoy the new slant that a little science can give to passages which will be familiar friends to many of us. Let's enjoy exploring God's good world.

Ruth M. Bancewicz

1
GOD AS FAITHFUL CREATOR

READ GENESIS 9:8–11 (NRSV)

> *Then God said to Noah and to his sons with him, 'As for me, I am establishing my covenant with you and your descendants after you and with every living creature that is with you, the birds, the domestic animals, and every animal of the earth with you, as many as came out of the ark. I establish my covenant with you, that never again shall all flesh be cut off by the waters of a flood, and never again shall there be a flood to destroy the earth.'*

This passage describes God making a covenant with 'every living creature' and, as was common in the ancient world, it views these as including creatures inhabiting the skies (birds) and the land (domesticated and wild animals). The word here translated 'covenant' is used to describe a contract regulating the relationship between two parties. Throughout the Bible there are records of various covenants between God and human beings, alone or as families or nations. As Christians we are drawn into the new covenant, sealed by Jesus' life, death and resurrection. The covenant in Genesis 9 is unusual, because God here promises something to 'all flesh', that is animals and not just humans.

Why does God not just make a covenant with Noah and his descendants – or perhaps with the humans and their domesticated animals that provide them with items necessary for daily life? The more that biologists uncover of the natural world, the more they become aware of the interdependency within and among all living things. There are highly intricate and dynamic relationships within each living cell, between cells and between organs in bodies, and between animals and plants, both as individuals and as whole populations. We are part of a web of life. God did not create us in isolation but as creatures embedded within a wider created order. Moreover, here and elsewhere in the scriptures we find evidence of the Lord's ongoing faithfulness towards *all* that lives, not just humankind.

Thank you, Lord God, that you care for and continue to support all that you have made. Help us, Lord, to consider how we should live in relationship with your wider world in a way that respects you and all your creation.

Cherryl Hunt, former Biologist, Theologian and Theological Educator

2
GOD'S CREATURES

READ PSALM 104:10–24 (NIV)

> *He makes springs pour water into the ravines; it flows between the mountains. They give water to all the beasts of the field; the wild donkeys quench their thirst. The birds of the sky nest by the waters; they sing among the branches. He waters the mountains from his upper chambers… He makes grass grow for the cattle, and plants for people to cultivate… The lions roar for their prey and seek their food from God… How many are your works, Lord! In wisdom you made them all; the earth is full of your creatures.*

vv. 10–14, 21, 24

We might think of 'biology' and 'creation' as referring to two completely different ideas, but the Bible sees them woven together. In this theological poetry, all the creatures of the earth are God's creatures. All they eat and drink, just as all we ourselves eat and drink, comes ultimately from God.

And here there is no hint of a God who starts the universe off with a Big Bang, then withdraws to let the world care for itself. No, here is a God who is upholding and sustaining all biological diversity in all its richness at every moment. This is sometimes referred to as God's immanence in creation. Here we have an involved God, who makes the plants grow and who supplies the food for lions. The earth is full of God's creatures and the immense beauty and complexity of living things act as a constant reminder of God's wisdom in creation.

So what biologists are doing in their research is to understand how God's wonderful world of biological diversity functions. Everything is connected. Everything that lives depends on everything else, and this elegant interconnectedness is brilliantly described in Psalm 104. The scope of biological diversity and complexity is so vast that thousands of biologists around the world still struggle to understand how it all works.

'How many are your works, Lord!' Sadly, those works are considerably less in number since humanity has caused the extinction of so many. Diversity loss due to human environmental abuse is tragic, because this entails the loss of God's creatures. Because all the creatures of the world are God's creatures, this is a vivid reminder for us that we are to care for the world of biological diversity as God intended.

Dear Lord, we thank you for your constant upholding of every living thing in the world, however big or small. Help us to be better carers of your wonderful creation.

Denis Alexander, Emeritus Director, The Faraday Institute for Science and Religion

3
GOD'S GOOD CREATION

READ JOB 38:1–16 (NIV)

> 'Where were you when I laid the earth's foundation? Tell me, if you understand. Who marked off its dimensions? Surely you know! Who stretched a measuring line across it? On what were its footings set, or who laid its cornerstone – while the morning stars sang together and all the angels shouted for joy?… The earth takes shape like clay under a seal; its features stand out like those of a garment… Have you journeyed to the springs of the sea or walked in the recesses of the deep?'

vv. 4–7, 14, 16

God is addressing Job, who had been through a terrible time, losing his wealth, health and all ten of his children. Job just wanted God to explain why the world could be so tough.

God's response is simply to point to the magnificence of creation which lies all around. Job 38—41 beautifully explains God's immense creativity, his power and his sovereignty. Every single thing in the entire universe was called into being by God himself, from the vastness of the stars to the smallest details of the birth of every baby goat (Job 39:1–3). Even the food the animals and birds eat is under God's sovereign care (Job 38:39, 41).

The earth is not just a random lump of rock hurtling through space: God himself is its creator. It is exactly the size he meant it to be. It is exactly where he meant it to be. Its mountains and valleys, its ocean depths and seas are just as he intended. And these things matter: they are what make the earth a habitable planet, a suitable home for people made in God's image.

I know as a geologist that if the earth had been a different size or a different distance from the sun or if it didn't have seas, mountains and valleys, it would almost certainly be a sterile, lifeless planet. We can thank God for his goodness in making such a wonderful home for us, one which God himself declared to be 'very good' (Genesis 1:31).

Lord God, I ask that today you will make me grateful for the wonderful world which you have created for us. Help us to use its resources to serve you and others. Amen.

Robert White, Emeritus Director, The Faraday Institute for Science and Religion, and Emeritus Professor of Geophysics, University of Cambridge

4
THE CREATIVE CREATION

READ GENESIS 1:20–24 (NRSV)

> *And God said, 'Let the waters bring forth swarms of living creatures, and let birds fly above the earth across the dome of the sky.' So God created the great sea monsters and every living creature that moves, of every kind, with which the waters swarm and every winged bird of every kind. And God saw that it was good. God blessed them, saying, 'Be fruitful and multiply and fill the waters in the seas, and let birds multiply on the earth'… And God said, 'Let the earth bring forth living creatures of every kind…' And it was so.*

This passage describes the participation of creation itself in the bringing into being of more life. God commands the waters to bring forth the fish, and this is followed by the earth being called upon to bring forth living creatures of every kind. In other words, he does not just bring creation into being but also empowers the earth and waters to bring forth more living things. Nor is the earth and waters' role limited: the waters bring forth every conceivable aquatic creature, from the biggest sea monsters to the smallest swarming things. The earth likewise brings forth every living creature of every kind in all their marvellous diversity.

But the cycle of creation does not stop there, for the newly created animals are themselves blessed by God and invited to participate in his gift of bringing new life into being. The call to humanity to be fruitful and multiply and fill the earth is much quoted, but it is preceded by the same blessing bestowed on the fish and the birds. In between the two blessings we have the creation of the living creatures and finally humans. Are we to imagine that the land animals are not blessed and invited to fill the earth? This seems inconceivable. All creation is invited to flourish together, and the cycle of procreation must continue until the earth and waters are teeming with life.

These verses encourage us to participate in God's continuing work of creation by enabling all creatures to flourish. Though the waters and soil might not spontaneously generate new life in a strictly literal sense, all living things are dependent on them. We must protect them from pollution and ensure space for God's 'good', vibrant and diverse creation to be fruitful and multiply as he intended.

Creator God, Help us to participate in your continuing work of creation by enabling all creatures to flourish and be fruitful as you intend.

Rebecca S. Watson, Lecturer and Director of Studies, Eastern Region Ministry Course, Cambridge

5

DISCERNING WISDOM THROUGH PLAYFUL, CHILDLIKE ENJOYMENT

READ PROVERBS 8:22–23, 30–31 (NIV)

> *Then I was constantly at his side. I was filled with delight day after day, rejoicing always in his presence, rejoicing in his whole world and delighting in the human race.*

vv. 30–31

The speaker in today's passage is Wisdom personified. Biblical wisdom is about alignment with God's creational intent. An analogy may help to explain. While it is possible to use a guitar to draw water from a well, it is unwise (the Bible would say 'foolish' or 'vain') to do so, as the guitar-maker intended it for making music. But adding percussive accompaniment to strumming (say, by knocking on the guitar with your knuckles) is a wise way to develop the instrument's potential. Made in the image of God, human beings are charged with discerning God's intention and wisely developing the huge potential built into God's creation.

Our passage speaks of the primacy of Wisdom, who was 'formed… at the very beginning'. Wisdom takes precedence over knowledge. Success in searching for knowledge through science and other endeavours does not guarantee discerning the way of Wisdom: knowledge can, and often is, used unwisely. How, then, is humanity to learn to discern Wisdom's way?

The Hebrew behind the phrase 'I was constantly at his side' is obscure. Some scholars suggest the translation 'I was a little child'. Moreover, 'rejoicing' translates a word that carries the connotation of playfulness. So Wisdom, the little child at the creator's side, laughs playfully as the panorama of creation unfolds in front of her. When my own children were very young, I noticed they often reacted with playful laughter as they encountered new facets of the world. An excellent way for us adults to school ourselves in discerning the way of Wisdom is to recover, maintain and cultivate a childlike, playful enjoyment of the wonder, diversity and intricacies of creation.

God our creator, who created the universe in wisdom, instil in us a sense of playful enjoyment of all your works. Amen.

Wilson Poon, Professor of Natural Philosophy, The University of Edinburgh

6
PRAISEWORTHY

READ PSALM 148:5–6, 13–14 (NIV)

> *Let them praise the name of the Lord, for at his command they were created, and he established them forever and ever – he issued a decree that will never pass away… Let them praise the name of the Lord, for his name alone is exalted; his splendour is above the earth and the heavens. And he has raised up for his people a horn, the praise of all his faithful servants, of Israel, the people close to his heart. Praise the Lord.*

This psalm begins and ends with 'Hallelujah' (translated in the NIV as 'Praise the Lord'), an exhortation to praise God. Everything from the highest reaches of heaven to the smallest creatures on earth is called to praise its creator. Three questions arise. Why praise? How can inanimate objects or animals praise anyone? What is praise, anyway?

Two reasons for praise are suggested by the writer. The first (vv. 5–6), after the call upon everything in the heavens, recalls the opening chapter of Genesis that declared that the sun, moon and stars were created by God, implying that they were not themselves deities to be worshipped, as was the practice of some religions. Written from the perspective of ancient cosmology, with waters above a solid dome or firmament, the poem nonetheless expresses the truth that the universe obeys law, i.e. the decree of verse 6 'that will never pass away'. The resulting regularity and order make possible the science that enhances our vision of the immensity of the universe. Coming down to earth, we see a diverse, interdependent creation, each living creature in its environment, the ecology revealed by our modern scientific perspective.

The second reason (vv. 13–14) reiterates that there is only one creator who gives strength, a symbolic horn, to his people. He is not the remote deist god, the god of the philosophers, but the God of Abraham, Isaac and Jacob, concerned for every human, from kings to women and children, and before whom all are equal.

But how do stars, sea creatures or snowflakes praise God? Just by being what they are – showing power, life and beauty in splendid and wonderful variety. They not only show God's power and glory, as affirmed by Psalm 19:1–4 and Romans 1:20, but they are instruments in his hand and under his control (Luke 8:22–24). The inscription on the tomb of Sir Christopher Wren in St Paul's Cathedral, which he designed, reads '*Si monumentum requiris circumspice*' – If you seek his memorial, look around you.

So, with vision enhanced also by science, seeing God in his artwork and action in creation, we see what praise is. Praise is not limited to singing complimentary songs about God, acknowledging his character; it is also what creation does simply by existing. If you want to see what praise is, look around you.

Our Father, help us to see you in the beauty of your wonderful creation and by your grace may others see you in us. Amen.

Paul Ewart, Emeritus Professor, Department of Physics, University of Oxford

7
REST

READ GENESIS 2:1–3 (NIV)

> *Thus the heavens and the earth were completed in all their vast array. By the seventh day God had finished the work he had been doing; so on the seventh day he rested from all his work. Then God blessed the seventh day and made it holy, because on it he rested from all the work of creating that he had done.*

Have you ever seen something so beautiful, so wonderful, that it took your breath away? You literally found yourself lost for words. It's not a new experience. We share it with people through the ages, both those who have faith and those who have none. Rather than taking away from this breathless sense of wonder, the view of heaven and earth that science provides deepens it. Microscopes and telescopes give sight beyond natural human senses, opening up the 'vast array' of creation from the smallest to the largest scales – a divine window.

Perhaps before heaven and earth, God too was lost for words. On each day of creation, God speaks. His word brings all things into being. Now, on the seventh day, he contemplates all of creation, beyond even the rich view that God's gift of science provides. There is no more speaking needed. It is complete. God rests. God rests his voice, a holy moment.

With the seeming fullness of our lives, we have lost something of knowing this rest of God. We fear silence, filling our lives with noise through our smart devices. Yet, in sabbath silence, in those moments that take our words away, we share in the deep delight of God over all that he has spoken into being, including his delight over us.

Next time you see one of the beautiful images of creation that science gifts to us popping up on your smartphone, tablet or TV, share a moment of holy silence with God. He invites you to join his wordless delight over what he has made and to rediscover the value he places in all things – and the value he places in you.

Praise to you, creator God, for the wonder of creation. Thank you for sharing it with me. In the vastness of it all, help me to know you more and to know that you know me. Amen.

Dave Gregory, Baptist Missioner for Science and Environment, Baptist Union Environment Network Convener, former Climate Scientist

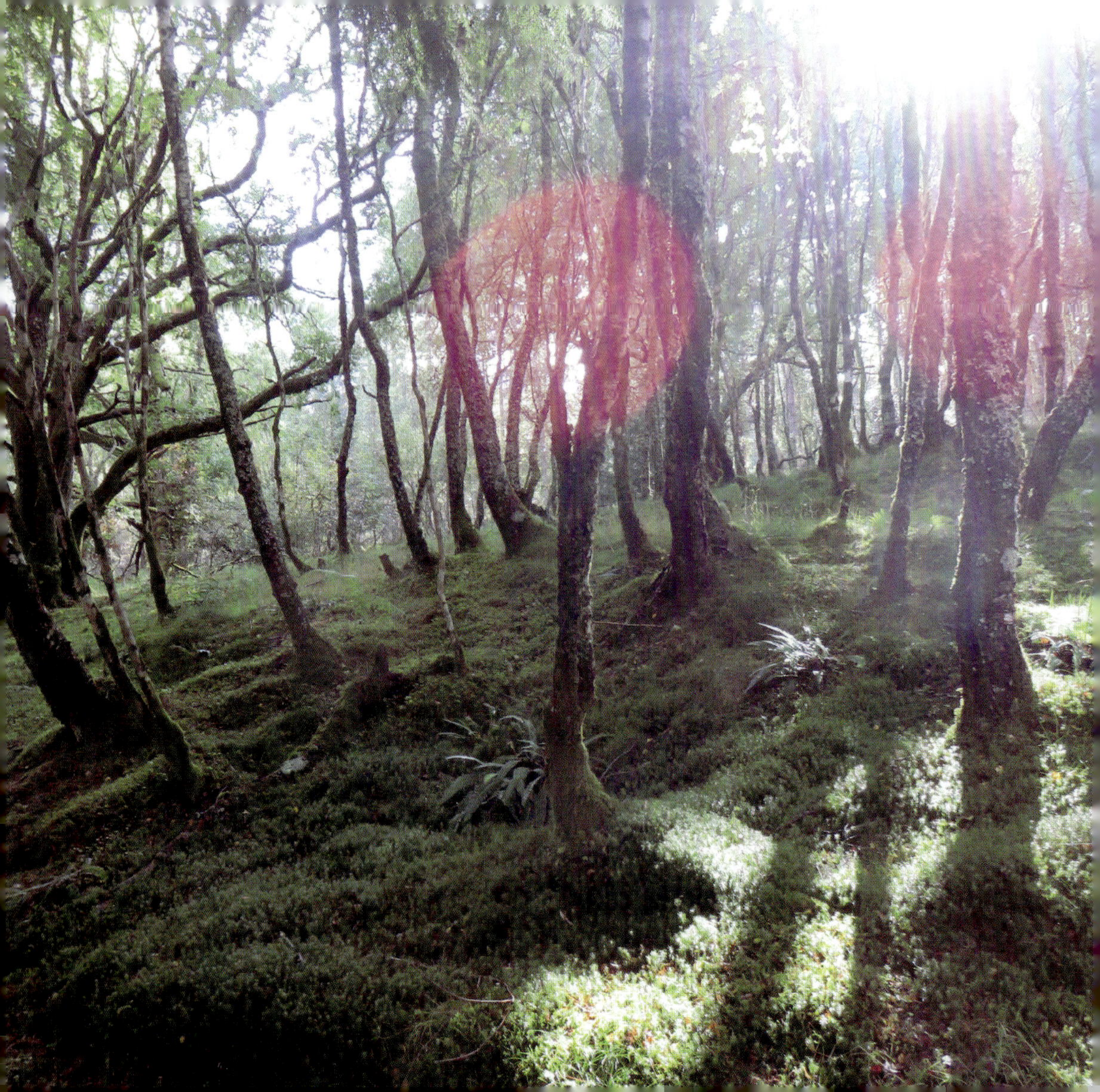

PART II

CHRIST AND CREATION

Discussions about science and Christianity can at times centre around a 'God' figure, losing sight of the Trinity. In reality, all three persons of God were, and still are, present in creation. Christ is the one through whom all things were made, as the first passage in this series reminds us. He also sustains all things. The next five devotions explore that theme, encouraging us to remember Christ as we explore his creation.

Ruth Bancewicz

Opposite: temperate rainforest, Applecross Peninsula, west coast of Scotland

8
NEW BEGINNINGS

READ JOHN 1:1–5 (NIV)

> *In the beginning was the Word, and the Word was with God, and the Word was God. He was with God in the beginning. Through him all things were made; without him nothing was made that has been made. In him was life, and that life was the light of all mankind. The light shines in the darkness, and the darkness has not overcome it.*

Modern science can tell us a great deal about the beginning. We certainly know when the earth formed and even when the universe formed. We also know a great deal about how they formed. For example, the Large Hadron Collider lies beneath the border of Switzerland and France, near Geneva, occupying a tunnel some 27 km in circumference, and it is one of the world's largest physics experiments, designed to help us understand what happened at the beginning of the universe. Equally, the return of material from the asteroid Bennu in 2023, a journey that lasted two years and over two million kilometres, may hold clues to the earliest origins of our solar system.

John gives us another angle on the beginning. It reminds us of the ancient story of Genesis, about a God purposefully and lovingly creating his world. The regular use of these verses in Christmas carol services reminds us that this is also the beginning of a new story, albeit connected to the ancient one. The new story is one of light shining into what sadly had become a darkened world and a place in which God's best purposes had become frustrated. This is a story of light challenging and overcoming the darkness around it.

This is also the story of God's creative word making possible a work of re-creation and a new beginning. As we continue into John's gospel we read how the one who in the beginning formed life is now the author of new life. This is important for those times when we long for a new beginning for ourselves or those close to us. In my work as a geochemist, I have observed some of the earliest traces of life on earth, formed 3.7 billion years ago – the original 'beginning' if you will. John is telling us that in God's new creative order, even more exciting new beginnings are possible.

Thank you, Lord, for the possibility of a new beginning, for myself and those around me.

Hugh Rollinson, Emeritus Professor of Earth Sciences, University of Derby

9
CHRIST THE CREATOR

READ HEBREWS 1:2–3 (NIV)

> *In these last days he has spoken to us by his Son, whom he appointed heir of all things, and through whom also he made the universe. The Son is the radiance of God's glory and the exact representation of his being, sustaining all things by his powerful word. After he had provided purification for sins, he sat down at the right hand of the Majesty in heaven.*

We now know that the universe contains billions of galaxies, each of which contains billions of stars. The numbers are overwhelming. Today's passage tells us that Christ made them all – the entire universe is his; he made it, and it belongs to him. There are also billions of species of plants, animals and insects on earth. Again, Christ made them all – every part of the universe belongs to him. 'Without him nothing was made that has been made' (John 1:3).

Not only did he create the universe, but he also keeps it all going, sustaining everything for every moment of every day, and he has been doing so ever since the beginning of time. Jesus, the second person of the Trinity, didn't inherit the universe; he made it, and he, the maker, is the same Christ who chose to die to redeem us from our sins.

All this shows God's glory. We see the radiance of his character in the overwhelming greatness of the universe: his concern for every detail, even the parts that human eyes will never see. God spoke the universe into being, and God's same powerful word sustains every part of the universe. He could write off his creation, but in his love he chooses to sustain it moment by moment, showing his gracious love, power and authority.

The one who spoke the world into being and sustains it day-to-day is the same one who speaks to us. He also created us and saved us. So we can trust him to sustain us, just as he takes care of the rest of his creation.

Thank you, God, that you have created this wonderful world that shows your glory. Thank you that I can trust you to care for me.

Keith Fox, Emeritus Professor of Biochemistry, University of Southampton

10

EVIDENCE AND THE SUPREMACY OF CHRIST

READ COLOSSIANS 1:15–17, 19 (NRSV)

> *He is the image of the invisible God, the firstborn of all creation, for in him all things in heaven and on earth were created, things visible and invisible, whether thrones or dominions or rulers or powers – all things have been created through him and for him. He himself is before all things, and in him all things hold together… For in him all the fullness of God was pleased to dwell.*

The Christian faith is encapsulated in these stunning verses. Through Jesus' life, death and resurrection, all things – everything in the world as well as human beings – can be in a close relationship with God. But does the supremacy of Christ mean we should be able to obtain evidence of God's presence in the world? Although

Evidence and the supremacy of Christ

looking for this evidence was the expressed intention of early scientists, today the world can be almost completely described with the knowledge of science and mathematics alone.

But there is no need to give up looking for the evidence for God; instead, we need to redefine what we mean by 'evidence'. The word 'science' comes from the Latin *scientia*, meaning 'to know', whereas the biblical word associated with knowledge is 'wisdom', which is more about how we use what we know to interpret the world around us.

If we look at the complexity of our world (perhaps the vastness of the universe or the intricacies of the insect world – anything really), we can reach for some scientific facts. But if we contemplate the world with the wisdom of the supremacy of Christ, then startling new evidence emerges – our experience of wonder, joy and awe when we are faced with the world uncovered by science. And this is the evidence we need to know the truth that all things in heaven and on earth are held together in God through Jesus Christ our Lord. Our awe at the evolution of species, our wonder at the organisation of ant societies – whatever it might be – this is the evidence that leads to deeper wisdom than facts can ever deliver. Christ is supreme over all the earth!

Creator God, grant me the wisdom to wonder and the faith to know that Christ reigns supreme today in my life and everywhere.

Gillian Straine, Priest, Scientist and CEO of The Guild of Health and St Raphael

11
POWERFUL

READ LUKE 8:22–25 (NRSV)

> *One day he got into a boat with his disciples, and he said to them, 'Let us go across to the other side of the lake.' So they put out, and while they were sailing he fell asleep. A windstorm swept down on the lake, and the boat was filling with water, and they were in danger. They went to him and woke him up, shouting, 'Master, Master, we are perishing!' And waking up, he rebuked the wind and the raging waves; they ceased, and there was a calm. Then he said to them, 'Where is your faith?' They were terrified and amazed and said to one another, 'Who then is this, that he commands even the winds and the water and they obey him?'*

Some of Jesus' disciples had lived all their lives on the shores of the Sea of Galilee. Although they wouldn't have been able to explain the science behind it, they would have relied on their knowledge of the local weather to keep safe. We now know that it is the cold air sweeping down from nearby mountains that whips up sudden storms on this relatively enclosed and low-lying body of water. When Jesus invited the disciples to cross the lake, did a few of them murmur between themselves that the weather didn't look quite right for such a trip, or was the squall that suddenly blew in a surprise even to the seasoned sailors?

Luke seems to use the word 'Master' (rather than 'Teacher') when the disciples don't understand what Jesus is doing. The disciples were supposed to trust Jesus – but how? Did he expect them to calm the storm themselves, or was he disappointed that they were so amazed when he brought about calm? Did he mind that they asked for help in such a desperate way, or would he rather they just keep bailing and trust that they would be kept safe – as Jesus did while he slept? Most of the commentators I consulted opted for one or other of the latter two options – that they should have trusted Jesus more and been a bit less desperate.

In the end, 'He who was sleeping was awakened and sent the sea into a sleep' (Ephrem the Syrian). Miracles don't have to defy science. In fact, knowing how something works can make a miracle all the more awe-inspiring. A meteorologist or sailor might be able to describe how a squall could leave as suddenly as it arrived, but that needn't explain away what Jesus did. The wonder was that the wind appeared to instantly obey Jesus' rebuke. The disciples might have seen a number of such 'coincidences' (or miracles of timing) by this point, but this one was the most surprising so far. With their knowledge of Galilean weather, they were well equipped to recognise Jesus' extraordinary authority over creation. What's more, they had just seen their teacher exercise the same power that they had learned, through scripture, is characteristic of the God of Israel. No wonder they were afraid!

Father God, help us to trust you even in the most testing circumstances. Help us to remember your power and pray before we panic. Amen.

Ruth M. Bancewicz, Church Engagement Director, The Faraday Institute for Science and Religion

12
CHOOSING GOOD TREES

READ MATTHEW 7:13–14, 16b–18 (NIV)

> 'Do people pick grapes from thorn-bushes, or figs from thistles? Likewise, every good tree bears good fruit, but a bad tree bears bad fruit. A good tree cannot bear bad fruit, and a bad tree cannot bear good fruit.'

vv. 16b–18

Walking under a bright, pale blue, cloudless winter sky, my eyes were drawn to a barren tree, stripped of its leaves by autumn storms and winter frosts, yet still majestic, silhouetted against the sky. Amazingly, the same patterns crop up in nature time and time again. The pattern of the branches is like that of the airways of our lungs. Trees are truly the lungs of the earth, controlling the level of carbon dioxide in the atmosphere, sustaining the vast range of life that God declared to be very good.

We aren't always good at recognising good from bad trees, though. We cut down many of the world's natural forests that support a diverse range of life beneath their shady canopy. We replace them with bad trees that quickly suck the goodness out of the soil, limiting the fruitfulness of the living world.

When it comes to caring for creation, we have not always followed a narrow path that keeps in step with God's command to Adam to 'till and keep' the fruitful garden of Eden (see Genesis 2:15, NRSV). We have carved a wide one, destructive of God's earth and the life that shares it with us. And we feel the consequences of global warming: forest fires, floods, coastlines washed away. Jesus' words seem to be coming true before our very eyes:

> 'Everyone who hears these words of mine and does not put them into practice is like a foolish man who built his house on sand. The rain came down, the streams rose, and the winds blew and beat against that house, and it fell with a great crash.'
> MATTHEW 7:26–27

Yet Jesus' words also bring hope. Changing our lives – how we travel, what we eat, how we use energy, protecting good trees – means we build on firmer foundations. It is possible to walk the narrow path that leads to life as we listen to his word and do 'the will of my Father who is in heaven' (v. 21) for the earth, its peoples and its creatures.

Creator God, your trees sustain the breath of life that fills my lungs. Help me to play my part in sustaining their life. Amen.

Dave Gregory, Baptist Missioner for Science and Environment, Baptist Union Environment Network Convener, former Climate Scientist

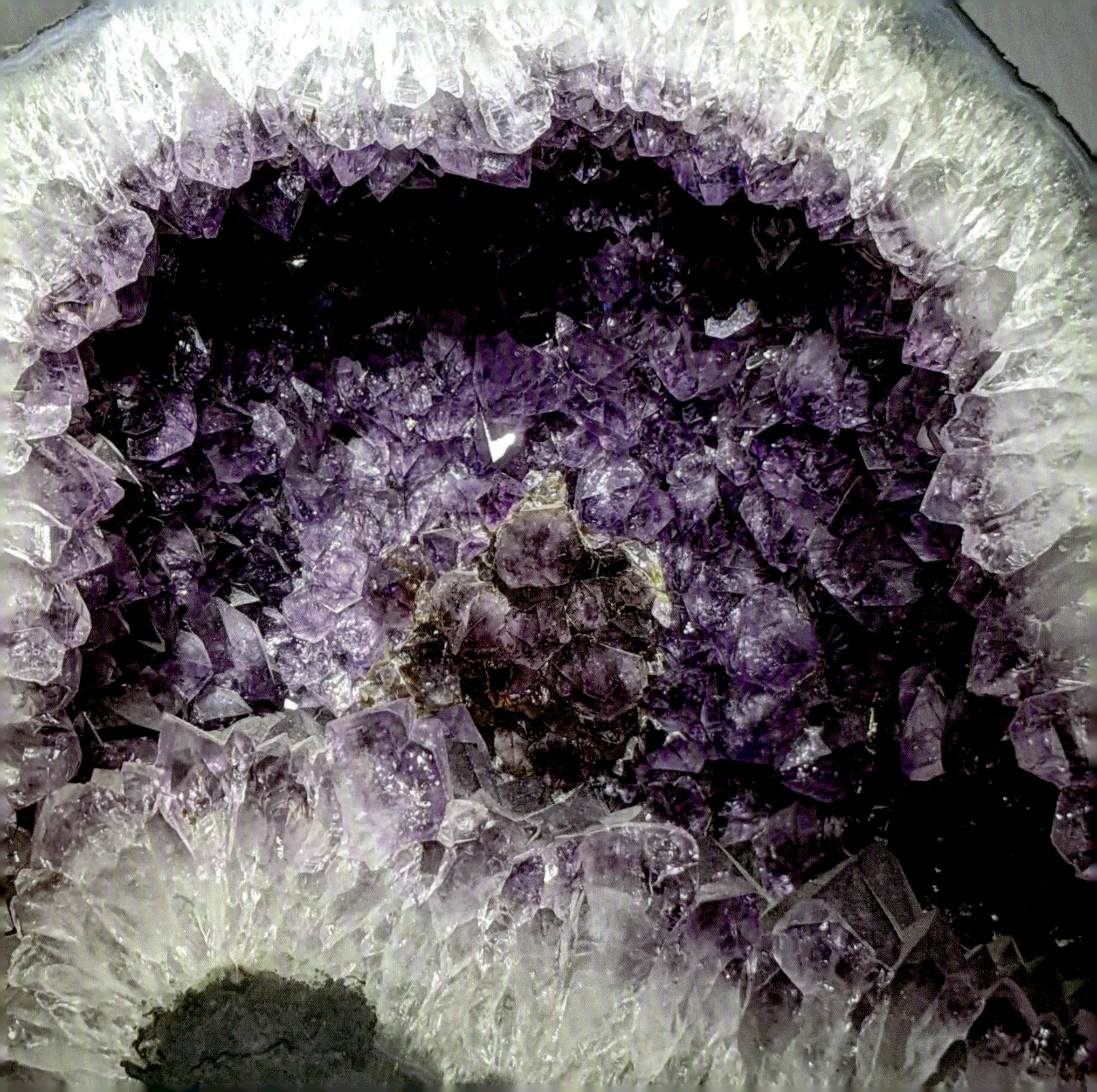

PART III

EXPLORING CREATION

We inhabit an incredible planet, where great beauty, fruitfulness and diversity can be found even in the most surprising places. An ordinary urban garden, railway embankment or field edge may contain countless species of insects, plants and microbes. Deep-sea vents or subterranean caves can be bursting with life. We benefit from creation in countless ways, including food, drink, clothing, medicine, building materials and relaxation. There is also a messy side to the non-human world – a wildness that we have to learn to live alongside, as well as the pain, disease and environmental destruction that can result from our own broken relationship with the created order.

Opposite: a geode (crystal-lined hollow rock) continuing amethyst and pyrite

In this section, we will work through some of the familiar passages on creation that are scattered throughout the Old Testament, but with a different slant. Each writer has shared some of their own heart for a particular area of scientific exploration in a way that helps unpack the meaning of the passage.

I hope you find these studies encouraging and uplifting, expanding your mind to take in a little more of the God of the whole universe and his creative attributes.

Ruth M. Bancewicz

13
DELIGHTING IN BOUNTIFUL CREATION

READ PSALM 111:2–5 (NIV)

> *Great are the works of the Lord; they are pondered by all who delight in them. Glorious and majestic are his deeds, and his righteousness endures forever. He has caused his wonders to be remembered; the Lord is gracious and compassionate. He provides food for those who fear him; he remembers his covenant forever.*

Many of the psalms, including Psalm 111, reveal the majesty of God and the grandeur of his work within creation. What God has done is evidenced in the world he spoke into being. His glory is shown and his works are remembered.

I live in a tropical climate with an abundance of fruit from the land. One of my delights is food that grows on trees and bushes. I think about the beauty of leaves and flowers in bloom that eventually turn into edible fruit for human and non-human creatures.

These fruits are tangible reminders of how God feeds his creation from the land. A direct connection between creator and creation.

I love the *aratiles* berries that grow on a tree across the street from where I live. Whenever I walk by and pick some of its berries, I savour the pops of subtle sweetness and wonder about other creatures – children, birds and bats – who also enjoy its bounty at different times. I also ponder about the creator who designed these edible jewels along with the range of other fruits in this region.

God's design is that creation helps sustain creation. How amazing that God provides food for his creatures from within creation itself. And not just any kind of food; it's good food!

Another one of my favourite regional fruits is a wild citrus called *biasong*. Its citrusy zing helps to lift the flavour of any dish I prepare, especially fish and salads. But I'm reminded that before the *biasong* ends up in my kitchen, these fruits first mature on a tree next to its just-as-fragrant leaves. And this tree is rooted in soil from which a lot of other food grows.

The God who provided manna and quail for the Israelites in the wilderness is the same God who feeds the community of creation where I live in Asia. God demonstrates grace and compassion as he provides for our daily needs from within creation.

Delighting in bountiful creation 47

Through the food we eat, we are reminded about the interrelationships in the created world. Creatures do not exist in isolation from one another; rather, we relate dynamically and depend on each other for survival. We are designed for loving relationships with creator and creation.

As the psalmist declares God's great works, how do we connect to the heart of our maker and express our love for creation?

Lord Jesus, may we truly taste and see that you are good! May we use our full senses to know you more through your created world – even in the food we eat.

Jasmine Kwong, Creation Care Advocate, with an interest in food security and marine conservation

14
ON THE OCEAN

READ PSALM 104:24–30 (NIV)

> *How many are your works, Lord! In wisdom you made them all; the earth is full of your creatures. There is the sea, vast and spacious, teeming with creatures beyond number – living things both large and small. There the ships go to and fro, and Leviathan, which you formed to frolic there. All creatures look to you to give them their food at the proper time. When you give it to them, they gather it up; when you open your hand, they are satisfied with good things. When you hide your face, they are terrified; when you take away their breath, they die and return to the dust. When you send your Spirit, they are created, and you renew the face of the ground.*

One privilege of being an oceanographer, going 'to and fro' on the sea, is experiencing the grandeur of God's creation. On a research trip in the Atlantic we once encountered a force 11 storm with 12-metre (40-foot) waves, evoking Jesus and his disciples' experience of a storm on the Sea of Galilee. As we were bouncing around rather uncomfortably in the large waves, a pod of pilot whales came and played in the waves breaking around our ship. This brought to mind the verse in this psalm about God forming Leviathan (a large sea creature) to frolic in the sea. The whales were ideally adapted to their environment and enjoying being in it.

This psalm reminds us that not only did God create the creatures in the sea, echoing Genesis, but that he also cares for and provides for them. The sea does indeed teem with life, as the psalm says and as shown in the BBC TV series *Blue Planet*. God is sovereign over all the creatures in the sea, both giving them life and taking it away. Their lives are dependent on his provision of food for them at the proper time. Likewise, we too are dependent on God both for life and for food. It can be easy to forget at times that God is our provider, too.

God my provider, as your other creatures do, help me to look to you for everything I need.

Meric Srokosz, Professor of Physical Oceanography, National Oceanography Centre, Southampton, and former Associate Director, The Faraday Institute for Science and Religion

15
TRANSCENDENCE

READ PSALM 148:7–12 (NRSV)

> *Praise the Lord from the earth, you sea monsters and all deeps, fire and hail, snow and frost, stormy wind fulfilling his command! Mountains and all hills, fruit trees and all cedars! Wild animals and all cattle, creeping things and flying birds! Kings of the earth and all peoples, princes and all rulers of the earth! Young men and women alike, old and young together!*

Psalm 148 is a wonderful hymn, in which all areas of creation are called on to praise the Lord. God is deserving of the praise of all creation, and all creation is able to offer praise. In some traditions, worship is understood to be the saying of prayers or the singing of hymns or worship songs – exclusively human activities. Psalm 148 shows us just how wrong that understanding is.

By being the creatures that God intended and by filling the world with beauty and wondrous diversity, the rest of creation is also able to praise God. Animals offer praise when they delight in their surroundings and in just being themselves. Inanimate creation, too, offers praise by being a testament to God's creating love.

Nature also assists us in our own praise of God. Nature can inspire feelings of awe and wonder, and psychological research has shown that experiencing such feelings can produce a sense of transcendence – connecting with something bigger than ourselves. For Christians, such experiences can move us to greater praise of God. Science gives us an added way to experience awe and wonder as we explore the vastness of creation across the universe; as we marvel at the complexity of the microscopic world; as disciplines like psychology and genetics teach us more about what it means to be human.

Praise is something we do in community – rich and poor, men and women, old and young, human and non-human creation together. The mutual flourishing and peace of all creation is true praise to the loving creator.

Lord, teach me to marvel at your love, that my life may join with all creation in praising you. Amen.

Jennifer Brown, Church of England Priest, Social Psychologist of Religion, and Director of Training, The College of Preachers

16
ECOSYSTEMS AND BIODIVERSITY

READ GENESIS 9:12–17 (NIV)

> *And God said, 'This is the sign of the covenant I am making between me and you and every living creature with you, a covenant for all generations to come: I have set my rainbow in the clouds, and it will be the sign of the covenant between me and the earth.*

vv. 12–13

It is perhaps surprising to see how broad God's covenant with Noah is, for it not only encompasses Noah's family and his descendants, but also 'every living creature' – birds, domesticated animals and even the wild animals that might otherwise be seen as a threat. We don't often focus on God's care for animals, and yet mammals, birds and reptiles have lived on land for at least the last 200 million years and forms of marine life for much longer. No wonder animals have a special place in God's thinking, even to the point at which they are part of the worshipping community of heaven (Revelation 4:8).

And yet we live in times of crisis. The UK government's 2021 report *The Economics of Biodiversity: The Dasgupta Review* states: 'Biodiversity is declining faster than at any time in human history.' In the foreword to this report, David Attenborough writes: 'Today, we ourselves, together with the livestock we rear for food, constitute 96% of the mass of all mammals on the planet. Only 4% is everything else. We are destroying biodiversity, the very characteristic that until recently enabled the natural world to flourish so abundantly.' A number of recent authors have highlighted that it is our modern patterns of consumption that are the root of this decline; these are manifest in our approaches to land use (for food production) and climate change (our demand for cheap energy).

So how does this square with our reading from Genesis and God's declared covenant commitment of care for the whole animate world, 'every living creature'? We have God's promise that never again will all life be destroyed, reaffirming the original importance of animal life on earth as an essential part of God's creation. This promise has the whole character of God behind it – this is a promise that cannot be broken – as is confirmed by the sign of the rainbow. Further, this is a promise for all generations (v. 12) and so is just as relevant in our times as it was in the days of Noah.

Today we see God's concern for biodiversity loss being worked out through those groups and governments seeking to protect the natural environment. In 2020 I visited a farm in South Africa where the (Christian) farmer is seeking to reintroduce on to his land the world's most illegally trafficked animal – the pangolin. Closer to home are Christian organisations such as A Rocha working to fulfil God's re-creation mandate found in today's verses.

Lord, enlarge my vision to understand your love for the whole of your creation and help me to feel something of your pain in the face of its ongoing destruction.

Hugh Rollinson, Emeritus Professor of Earth Sciences, University of Derby

17
USING CREATION TO HEAL

READ REVELATION 4:9–11 (NLT)

> *The twenty-four elders fall down and worship the one sitting on the throne…*
> *'You are worthy, O Lord our God, to receive glory and honour and power. For*
> *you created all things, and they exist because you created what you pleased.'*

vv. 10–11

The elders' worship here is a model for how we might worship – giving thanks to the Lord for his creation. There is much in the world around us that is beautiful, awe-inspiring and good. This passage inspires me to think of natural phenomena worth giving thanks for.

Have you ever had a broken bone? You may have had an X-ray or a CT scan to see what is going on inside your body. Perhaps you've had a muscular issue? X-rays aren't much good here, so you may have had an ultrasound or an MRI instead.

This seems like recent technology, but ultrasound and X-rays, in particular, already existed in nature. X-rays are high-energy light, invisible to the naked human eye. They were discovered accidentally by a physicist who soon saw their potential. Just weeks after the discovery, he captured the first known X-ray image: his wife's hand. Ultrasound is high-energy sound, so high-pitched that humans can't hear it. Dolphins and bats use such noises for communication and navigation. In fact, discovering how bats navigate was part of the journey in developing ultrasound technology.

The passage tells us that it pleased God to create phenomena like X-rays and ultrasound, a hidden jewel within creation for us to tease out, harness and use for the benefit of many. I find it truly awe-inspiring that we can use tools nestled within Christ's creation to explore, diagnose and heal. As the elders in Revelation proclaimed: God's handiwork is worthy of our praise.

In my worship I wonder: what other undiscovered treasures has God made for us to unearth?

Jesus, creator of the visible and invisible – thank you for all that you made. May you give us wisdom in how to use, explore and celebrate the world around us.

Davinder Gardner, Principal Clinical Scientist in Radiotherapy Physics and Co-Director of The Faith Experiment

Opposite: bone-building cells (osteoblasts)

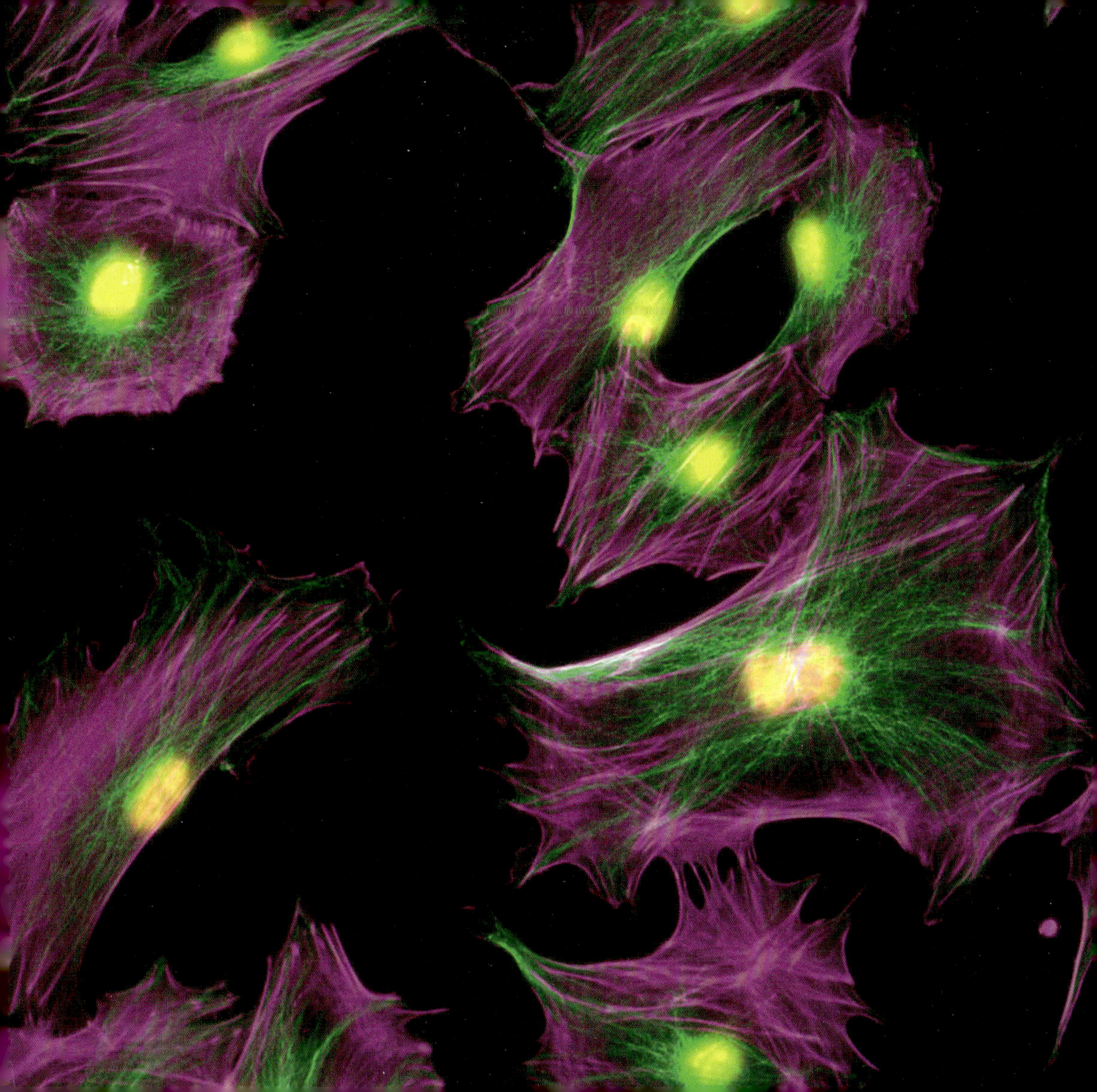

18
THROUGH THE TELESCOPE

READ PSALM 19:1–4 (NRSV)

> *The heavens are telling the glory of God, and the firmament proclaims his handiwork. Day to day pours forth speech, and night to night declares knowledge. There is no speech, nor are there words; their voice is not heard; yet their voice goes out through all the earth and their words to the end of the world.*

Some years ago, my wife and I were holidaying in Croatia. From our balcony in the evenings, because we were far away from artificial light, we were able to see the night sky in all its splendour and to count shooting stars. In ancient Israel, there also would have been no light pollution, and the night sky would have been equally spectacular.

The psalmist says that the heavens declare the glory of God. They are silent, yet metaphorically they speak loud and clear, and they speak to people 'through all the earth' – even if today we need to escape to the countryside to get a clearer view. They provide universally available testimony to God's glory.

The psalmist had a much more limited view of the cosmos than we do today. For example, like many in the ancient world he imagined the heavenly bodies set into a metal dome over the earth called the firmament. Now we know that the universe is utterly vast, maybe 93 billion light years in diameter. We also know that there are over 100 billion stars in our own Milky Way galaxy and over 100 billion galaxies in the observable part of the universe. By astronomical standards the sun is a very ordinary star, yet it is an 865,000-mile diameter nuclear furnace that has been radiating 400 trillion watts of power for many billions of years. Do these facts make me less or more in awe of God, the majestic creator of it all? Well, obviously, more so.

Our Christian faith teaches us that God, the creator of this unimaginably vast cosmos, is the very same God who, in the person of Jesus Christ, took human flesh and became a vulnerable baby. He came to achieve for us what we could not do for ourselves: by his perfect obedience, cross and resurrection, he redeemed us from all our failures. Now isn't that awesome?

As we understand ever more of your awe-inspiring creation, make us much more thankful, Father, for your vastly greater awe-inspiring care for us, shown in Christ. Amen.

Rodney Holder, Astrophysicist and Priest

19
IN THE LAB

READ PSALM 104:1, 10–18, 24–30 (NIV)

> *He makes springs pour water into the ravines… They give water to all the beasts of the field… The birds of the sky nest by the waters… He waters the mountains from his upper chambers; the land is satisfied by the fruit of his work.*

vv. 10–13

This psalm celebrates God's creation and begins with a call to worship the creator (v. 1). As a scientist, I study the world that God has created and my work is worship. If I separate my Christian faith and my secular work, then my work becomes dry and so does my soul. Isn't this true for any of us, whether our work is 'sacred' or 'secular', whether outside or inside the home, whether or not we receive a salary?

God not only created the earth and all its living creatures, but he also made the earth produce all that is required to sustain his creation. Notice the emphasis on abundant water, which is essential for all the plants and animals to survive (vv. 10–13). From there comes the grass for cattle to eat and plants for people to cultivate for food (v. 14). We now know that it is the green plants that capture carbon dioxide from the air which produces not only food, but also the oxygen we breathe.

Cultivating the fruit of the earth provides purpose and pleasure for humankind (vv. 10–15). The well-watered trees provide a nesting place for birds and the mountain crags provide a home for animals (vv. 16–18). God has provided the earth as a resource so that we and all his creatures can thrive. Do we treasure this? Do those of us who live in well-watered places show concern for those who are suffering the effects of man-made climate disaster?

As I study God's works in the lab, I am humbled by the richness of his wisdom and feel awe at the vastness and variety of his creation (vv. 24–26). We are completely dependent on God, both for the good things he gives us for practical day-to-day living (vv. 27–28) and for life (or death) itself (vv. 29–30). Do we acknowledge this in the way we live or do we separate sacred from secular?

Lord, thank you for the treasure trove of your wisdom. Guide us in our daily decisions, helping us to trust that you can see beyond the horizon.

Sarah Perrett, Associate Director, The Faraday Institute for Science and Religion, and Professor of Biochemistry, Chinese Academy of Sciences

20
GOD, THE TRUE MASTER CRAFTSMAN

READ EXODUS 31:1–5 (NLT)

> *Then the Lord said to Moses, 'Look, I have specifically chosen Bezalel son of Uri, grandson of Hur, of the tribe of Judah. I have filled him with the Spirit of God, giving him great wisdom, ability, and expertise in all kinds of crafts.'*

vv. 1–3

I love flying and dreamed of becoming a pilot growing up. I also admired great engineers like Sir Frank Whittle, the inventor of the turbojet engine that powers the aircraft we fly in today. I did not become a pilot, but I am now a materials engineer working for a metal-forging company that makes parts for aeroplanes and helicopters.

Before a part is forged, engineers design its geometry using computer software. Each part starts off as a simple block of metal, which is compressed into the desired shape by forging hammers or presses. Sometimes, a master forger will shape the metal manually, a task that requires a high degree of skill. The part is subsequently heated in a furnace and cooled to room temperature. This process allows the shuffling of layers of atoms in the metal to achieve an arrangement that makes the entire part strong and durable.

The invention of powerful machines has enabled us to achieve engineering feats that were not possible in previous centuries. While we often credit these advancements to human ingenuity, it is easy to forget that God is the one who gives humankind the ideas and skills required to make things, as shown in the verses above. The fact that God chose a certain man and endowed him with particular skills to make the tabernacle reveals his precise nature. This is demonstrated in the detailed construction of the tabernacle in Exodus 36. A few hundred years later, God equipped Solomon with the wisdom and resources to build the temple as a centre of worship, and its elaborate design made it one of the most magnificent buildings in the world at the time.

As modern-day technologies make knowledge acquisition more accessible, let us not forget that all gifts and talents come from God, which should inspire us to praise him.

Dear God, we praise and thank you for giving us so many different skills. Please help us to be good stewards of these gifts and to use them responsibly for the betterment of our communities. Amen.

Adriel Wong, Materials Engineer, Mettis Group

21
THROUGH THE MICROSCOPE LENS

READ JOB 9:4–10 (NIV)

> *His wisdom is profound, his power is vast. Who has resisted him and come out unscathed? He moves mountains without their knowing it and overturns them in his anger. He shakes the earth from its place and makes its pillars tremble. He speaks to the sun and it does not shine; he seals off the light of the stars. He alone stretches out the heavens and treads on the waves of the sea. He is the Maker of the Bear and Orion, the Pleiades and the constellations of the south. He performs wonders that cannot be fathomed, miracles that cannot be counted.*

We have all stared at the sky on a clear night and been awed by the sheer scale and beauty of the great array of stars above us. But we can be equally awe-inspired as we look at the very small – these days with the help of fancy microscopes. Our own bodies contain around ten trillion cells, of which around 100 billion are brain cells. And if you add up all the connections between those brain cells, that comes to something like 500 trillion. Our own brains are the most complex known structures in the universe. And like the stars, which die and are being formed every day, only numerically far more so, around 240 billion cells are being replaced in our bodies every day.

So just as Job writes, our creator God is an incredibly active creator. Job's insights are all in the present tense: God moves, shakes, speaks, stretches, makes and performs. God is no distant creator who gave the universe some laws back at the beginning to make things work properly, but then withdrew from the action like some absentee landlord. No, God is the one who is constantly creating and upholding everything that exists.

God's wisdom is profound, and God performs wonders that cannot be fathomed. Science is simply an attempt to describe and understand those wonders – but really we are only just beginning. So scientists do what Job was doing, describing the works of the constantly creating God, but using a more specialised language. Doing science for a Christian is an important aspect of their daily worship.

Lord, give us a fresh vision of your moment-by-moment upholding of your awe-inspiring creation.

Denis Alexander, Emeritus Director, The Faraday Institute for Science and Religion

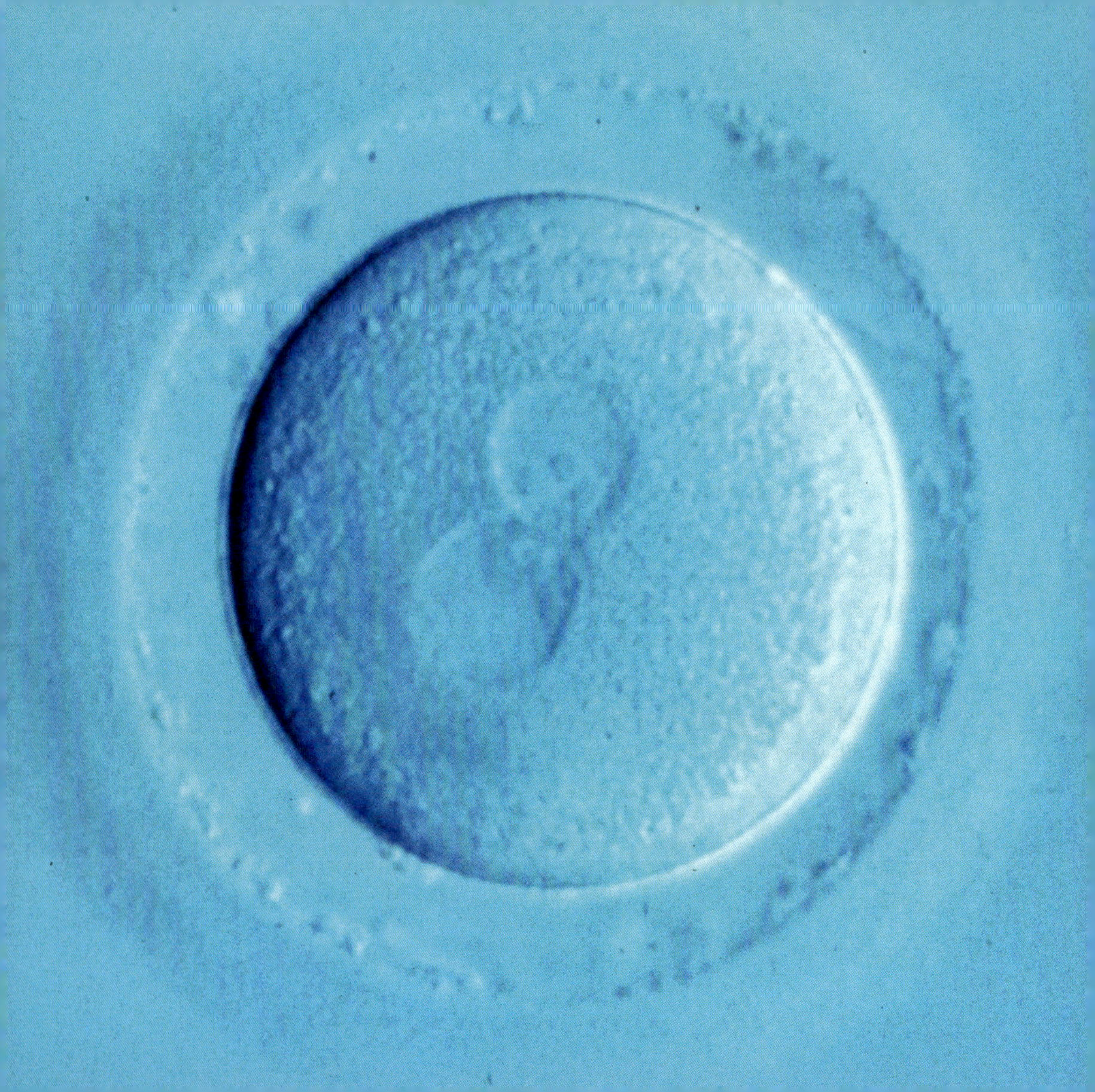

PART IV
BEING HUMAN

All of us have an important contribution to make to the body of Christ at every point in our lives, whether receiving or giving care or (more often) somewhere in between. Society does not always recognise this, and we can experience intense pressures to label or treat certain kinds of people as having more value than others. Throughout our journey we may also face difficult medical decisions, both for ourselves and for those we love, as well as the members of our churches.

We naturally turn to the Bible for encouragement that each person is of enormous value in God's eyes. We also look to scripture for answers to ethical decisions. When it comes to the big questions of modern medical ethics, however, the Bible has few

Opposite: a newly fertilised egg

detailed answers. Instead, we can find wisdom in its pages that we can apply in new situations.

This section looks at some of the most important questions and issues relating to the value of each person as an individual made in the image of God. The reflections relate to issues around the beginning and end of life and care for the vulnerable. Our hope is that they will help you to grow in your understanding of Christian bioethics and to identify biblical principles that can be applied in the opportunities and challenges that you face in the coming years.

Ruth M. Bancewicz

22
CARE FOR THE VULNERABLE

READ DEUTERONOMY 10:12–22 (NRSV)

> 'So now, O Israel, what does the Lord your God require of you? Only to fear the Lord your God, to walk in all his ways, to love him, to serve the Lord your God with all your heart and with all your soul, and to keep the commandments of the Lord and his decrees that I am commanding you today, for your own well-being… For the Lord your God is God of gods and Lord of lords, the great God, mighty and awesome, who is not partial and takes no bribe, who executes justice for the orphan and the widow, and who loves the strangers, providing them food and clothing. You shall also love the stranger, for you were strangers in the land of Egypt.'

vv. 12–13, 17–19

This passage highlights three classes of people who represent the socially vulnerable, powerless or marginalised. God's intention for the Israelites was that they should reflect his character of justice and mercy by taking care of these people in their midst. They were to live out the greatest commandments: to love both God and neighbour. One motivation for this behaviour was to come from deep within their own identity: the fact that God protected them and showed them justice when they were weak and powerless while in slavery in Egypt.

This ethic is the very opposite of what we are led to believe is the driving force behind the living world: the struggle against all others for survival. It's true that competition for limited resources is key for every organism, but cooperation is also an incredibly important and ignored factor. Every major evolutionary transition – from molecules to cells, simple cells to complex cells, single cells to multicellular organisms, individual organisms to pairs of parents, and pairs to communities – has been accompanied by a step-change in cooperation. At the very centre of your being, and of every living thing on the planet, are organic components working together to achieve greater ends than they could on their own.

Genuine altruism – the ability to make decisions that don't benefit (or indeed actively work against) oneself even in the broadest sense – seems to be a uniquely human trait. But the key importance of cooperation in the created order does resonate with the divine command to care for others. Creation reflects something of its maker.

A second motivation for justice and mercy given in this passage is less altruistic: 'for your own well-being' (v. 13). Today we know the benefits of behaving in altruistic ways: interacting with other people, helping others and working together can increase our own well-being, even to the extent of boosting the immune system and reducing stress levels.

The Israelites did not understand the world in a scientific way, but their God-given law underscored the link between the care for vulnerable and marginalised people and the well-being of the whole nation. As the biologist and philosopher Jeff Schloss has said: 'It looks like we're really built to flourish when we give and receive care for others.'

Father, help us to honour your intention for us by living in justice and mercy, especially when this costs us dearly. Amen.

Ruth M. Bancewicz, Church Engagement Director, The Faraday Institute for Science and Religion

23
THE IMAGE OF GOD

READ GENESIS 1:26–27 (NRSV)

| *Then God said, 'Let us make humans in our image, according to our likeness.'*
v. 26a

What it means for humans to be made in the image and likeness of God has been debated in Christian theology down the ages. Irenaeus distinguished between these terms, 'image' denoting our rational nature and 'likeness' our moral virtue. He believed that at the fall humans retained the image but lost the likeness. In contrast, both Luther and Calvin recognised typical Hebrew parallelism here, so that no such distinction should be drawn. Swiss theologian Emil Brunner took a view similar to Irenaeus. However, his colleague Karl Barth recognised the danger to which Brunner's interpretation could lead: those such as newborn children and adults who are not capable of exercising rationality or moral virtue could be rejected – a critically important matter during the Nazi period when the Barth–Brunner debate took place.

Certainly the rational interpretation needs some qualification. At the same time, it offers an explanation of the remarkable consonance between the human mind and the cosmos, the fact that we can do science and understand the laws that shape the universe, from the smallest subatomic particle to the furthest galaxy.

Barth's own interpretation of the *imago* is fundamentally relational and widely accepted today: 'He sets man in fellowship with Himself as a being existing in free differentiation and relationship'. It is this capacity for fellowship with God and with other humans that marks us as unique among God's creatures and distinguishes us from the animals.

Our passage says that God has given humans 'dominion' over all other living creatures on the earth, and this provides another interpretation of the *imago*. Here the Hebrew verb *rādā* means 'to rule' or, indeed, 'have dominion over'. It does not mean 'exploit', 'trash' or 'render uninhabitable'. Far from it. Bearing in mind the divine image that we bear, indicating the fellowship we enjoy with God and our human brothers and sisters, and that God's nature is 'love', we are to rule as God's vicegerents; in other words, to rule in his place and as he would rule.

Help us, Lord, to recognise your image in every person, and remove from us all conceit and prejudice, for Jesus' sake. Amen.

Rodney Holder, Astrophysicist and Priest

24
CARE FOR THE SUFFERING

READ MARK 2:23—3:6 (NRSV)

> *Again he entered the synagogue, and a man was there who had a withered hand. They were watching him to see whether he would cure him on the Sabbath, so that they might accuse him. And he said to the man who had the withered hand, 'Come forward.' Then he said to them, 'Is it lawful to do good or to do harm on the Sabbath, to save life or to kill?' But they were silent.*

vv. 3:1–4

These encounters, in all the synoptic gospels, form part of a series of confrontations between Jesus and Jewish religious authorities. Having been accused of blasphemy (2:1–12) and of eating with sinners (2:13–17), as well as quizzed about his attitude to laws around fasting (2:18–22), Jesus twice contravenes strict rules around behaviour on the sabbath (2:23—3:6). Jesus is under pressure – plots to kill him are afoot (3:6).

Care for the suffering 75

The middle sections in this barrage revolve around various aspects of eating, bracketed by accounts of restoration to health. The gospels depict Jesus performing a number of healing miracles, with a wide variety of beneficiaries. Women and men of a range of ages: some on the fringes of society (the blind beggar, those with leprosy); others, as here, God-fearing, respectable sabbath synagogue-attenders.

Not being in possession of full health is something which most of us will experience. Often this is only a temporary situation: recovery may come courtesy of our body's innate ability to heal or fight disease. Sometimes we require external assistance – thank God for antibiotics, prosthetics and surgery!

Health and well-being for all is prioritised in most societies. However, there is huge disparity in the resources available to achieve this: in developed countries, an average of more than US$4,000 per person is spent on healthcare each year, compared to only US$30 in the Democratic Republic of Congo. Even within affluent societies, there is a challenge in achieving equitable access to treatments, with the richest often able to 'queue-jump'. The lack of effective vaccine-sharing in the recent Covid-19 pandemic, leading to an estimated one million excess deaths in developing countries, is surely shameful.

Sometimes the challenges are about more than simply resource allocation. Our ability to intervene at the very beginning of life – with for example assisted reproductive technologies or prenatal diagnostics – can be helpful, but also presents ethical dilemmas as to the contexts in which they should be used. At the end of life, palliative care is often the ignored 'Cinderella' specialty, while debates rage around inappropriate interventions to prolong life and assisted dying.

We give thanks for advances in medical technologies, but long to see all people everywhere being able to live to their full potential.

Murdo Macdonald, Policy Officer, Church of Scotland Society, Religion and Technology

25
THE UNBORN CHILD

READ PSALM 139:13–16 (NRSV)

> *For it was you who formed my inward parts; you knit me together in my mother's womb. I praise you, for I am fearfully and wonderfully made. Wonderful are your works; that I know very well. My frame was not hidden from you, when I was being made in secret, intricately woven in the depths of the earth. Your eyes beheld my unformed substance. In your book were written all the days that were formed for me, when none of them as yet existed.*

From fertilisation to first breath – an amazing developmental journey from single cell to living infant. For the first few days, the tiny embryo is not yet attached to its mother. At around six days after fertilisation, the embryo implants into the wall of the uterus to establish a pregnancy and then starts to grow into a baby. (Note: in medical terminology, the embryo becomes a foetus early in pregnancy.) As a biologist, I understand a lot about this developmental process, but I continue to regard it – and the very precise way in which it is controlled – with awe. The psalmist can have known very little about how embryos/foetuses develop, but his poetic appreciation – 'I am fearfully and wonderfully made' – certainly hits the mark.

The pre-implantation embryo was completely unknown to biblical writers. However, this tiny ball of cells has become familiar to us because of IVF, in which the pre-implantation phase is equivalent in time to the passage of the early embryo down the fallopian tube. But how are we to regard these early embryos? In law they do not have the status of human persons. Some Christians disagree with this, suggesting that even one-cell embryos should be treated as persons. This would have significant implications for the practice of IVF, including the routine creation of 'spare' embryos and genetic diagnosis in order to reject embryos with particular genetic conditions.

Consideration of the foetus developing in the womb leads on to thinking about the deliberate termination of pregnancy. It is a topic that has divided and continues to divide Christians. Further, it also challenges our basis for ethical decision-making because the Bible is completely silent on abortion, although Exodus 21:22–25 suggests that foetuses were not valued as highly as people who are already born.

Psalm 139:13–16 is often quoted in support of prohibiting abortion, but surely cannot be read that way. As the conservative theologian and ethicist Richard B. Hays says of this passage: 'It must be interpreted within the poetic genre to which it belongs, not as a scientific or propositional statement.' Our decisions will have to be made not on the basis of specific 'rules', but on general principles applied with wisdom and compassion. We note that throughout scripture, a child is regarded as a gift from God and also that there is a general presumption in favour of life.

We thank you, God, and praise you for the beautiful and awesome complexity of the ways in which our bodies work. We praise you too for the renewal of life, generation after generation. We pray that all those who have to make decisions about human embryos and foetuses may do so with wisdom and compassion.

John Bryant, Professor Emeritus of Cell and Molecular Biology, University of Exeter

26
DISABILITY AND GENE EDITING

READ 2 CORINTHIANS 12:6–10 (NRSV)

> But if I wish to boast, I will not be a fool, for I will be speaking the truth. But I refrain from it, so that no one may think better of me than what is seen in me or heard from me, even considering the exceptional character of the revelations. Therefore, to keep me from being too elated, a thorn was given me in the flesh, a messenger of Satan to torment me, to keep me from being too elated. Three times I appealed to the Lord about this, that it would leave me, but he said to me, 'My grace is sufficient for you, for power is made perfect in weakness.' So I will boast all the more gladly of my weaknesses, so that the power of Christ may dwell in me. Therefore I am content with weaknesses, insults, hardships, persecutions, and calamities for the sake of Christ, for whenever I am weak, then I am strong.

Today's passage reflects on the apostle Paul's 'thorn in the flesh'. Many people think that this adversity refers to a bodily ailment, reminding us that there is more to life than physical perfection. God's will for our lives includes much more than good health, and God can work for his glory in circumstances that we might not choose. We thank God that scientific advances over the past hundred years have had dramatic effects on human health, including antibiotics, anti-cancer agents and drugs for treating mental illness. Scientists have even developed technologies for altering our genes (DNA), raising the possibility of curing genetic diseases. However, some people consider that this is a step too far, and that this is 'playing God'.

It is fraught with many ethical questions, but healing and restoration have always been part of Christian ministry. We should ponder Jesus' question: 'Is it lawful to do good or to do harm on the sabbath, to save life or to kill?' (Mark 3:4). We must not accept disease too readily with a misplaced fatalism that sees everything as God's will. There are many tragic genetic diseases that lead to early childhood death, for which arguments in favour of gene editing seem compelling. On the other hand, enthusiasm for gene editing can avoid questions of how society includes people with disabilities.

Paul's 'thorn in the flesh' reminds us that what seems like a disease and weakness may be a strength, and that God's 'power is made perfect in weakness' (v. 9). There is more to living a fulfilled life than physical ability. All people have worth, and we are precious because of who we are – made in God's image – not because of what we can or cannot do.

A common misconception is that improvements in health justify any intervention. However, there are many people whose strength comes from what seems like disease and weakness. Are we in danger of reinforcing an 'ableist' mentality, which assumes that independence and health should be maximised at all cost? An overzealous acceptance of gene editing can avoid questions of how we respect the people who regard their disabilities as alternative and equally valid ways of living. We all need to learn from these people.

So thank God for scientific advances that are part of God's way of alleviating human suffering. However, pray that these will be used responsibly, and honour those for whom God's grace and power is demonstrated in weakness.

Lord, I pray for scientists who work to treat disease, but thank you that you power can still be shown in my weakness.

Keith Fox, Emeritus Professor of Biochemistry, University of Southampton

27
END OF LIFE

READ GENESIS 25:7–10 (NRSV)

> *This is the length of Abraham's life, one hundred seventy-five years. Abraham breathed his last and died in a good old age, old and full of years, and was gathered to his people. His sons Isaac and Ishmael buried him in the cave of Machpelah, in the field of Ephron son of Zohar the Hittite, east of Mamre, the field that Abraham purchased from the Hittites. There Abraham was buried with his wife Sarah.*

Abraham had lived 100 years beyond the time when God called him to set out from Haran at the age of 75. God's promises of descendants and land were being fulfilled, and God's personal promise to Abraham of a long life ending peacefully (Genesis 15:15) was now realised. The time had arrived for Abraham to breathe his last breath. Hidden in this phrase is a reminder not so much of the interruption brought by death as the fact that every breath is a gift from our life-giving God. In each breath we take, God shows himself faithful.

Abraham's death is described in terms of homecoming – he was gathered to his people. God's promises looked beyond Abraham's life on earth; it was Abraham's time to go home – not to Haran, but to his people, the people of God. His homecoming was both physical and spiritual. His sons buried him in the place where he had lived (Genesis 13:18), the land he had bought to bury his wife Sarah (Genesis 23:10–18) and where later generations would follow (Genesis 49:29–32).

Whether or not Abraham's final days were uncomfortable, we are not told. We are told he was at peace: death held no power over him to trouble or frighten him. Abraham had learned to trust God's faithfulness: he was not surprised or unready to go home. He neither threw his life away nor clung to it with desperation. He had known this moment would arrive, though perhaps not exactly when. He had made the necessary practical arrangements and told his family what was to be done.

Abraham appears to have died with contentment, prepared in heart and spirit. His was a life well lived, despite some low points of his own making along the way. He valued life as a gift but understood that this part of his journey must end. He died with the certainty of God's promises continuing beyond his earthly life.

The lives of God's people are not given up in resignation to death but are given up in recognition of hope. Life is to be celebrated as a testimony to God's faithfulness in the past and anticipated with the joy in coming home to be with God, beyond the shadow of death under which we abide for now.

Loving heavenly Father, with thanks for your faithfulness in every day, we yearn for the glory and joy of living in your presence forever.

Andrew Perrett, GP

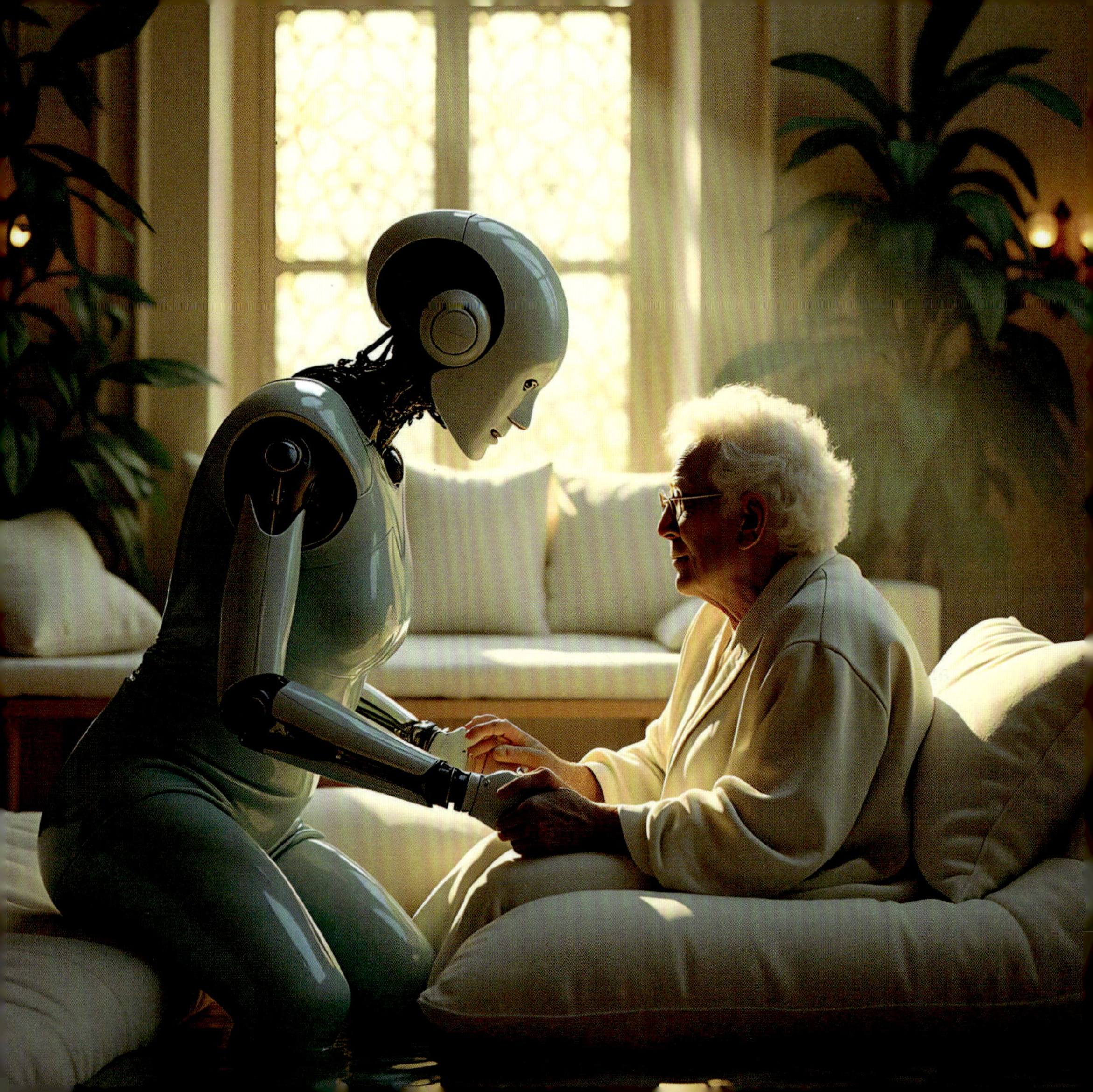

PART V

MORE THAN HUMAN?

Even if you are the greatest technophobe, it is worth recognising that everyone, everywhere is affected by artificial intelligence (AI). Whether going shopping or on a phone helpline, paying for parking or receiving healthcare, AI is already having an impact on your life and will increasingly do so in the coming years. Some of these technologies are extremely helpful. I am grateful that a chatbot can save me waiting half an hour to ask a simple question about my phone bill. On the other hand, I am concerned about the use of facial recognition software to track people's whereabouts in some countries.

As with most new technologies, the Bible has nothing to say about AI specifically, but much to say in general about how we use it. This section will equip you to think

Opposite: AI-generated image

about how AI affects our lives and how we can use or respond to it. We will also ask, how are other people affected and how can we speak up for them? How are the next generations using AI and how can we support them? We will explore broad biblical principles, such as being made in the image of God, idolatry, rest, the fall and what it means to be embodied. We will look at specific issues or aspects of human existence such as creativity, exercising power, kindness and counselling.

This next set of reflections bring different perspectives to this very new topic. Some are more cautious than others about the potential of AI to contribute to society in particular ways. No doubt Christian thinking on this subject will develop rapidly, and reflections like these will be very different in five or ten years' time. For now, I hope that they enlighten, challenge and inspire you.

Ruth M. Bancewicz

28
CROWNED WITH GLORY! GUIDED BY AI?

READ PSALM 8:3–8 (NIV)

> *When I consider your heavens, the work of your fingers, the moon and the stars, which you have set in place, what is mankind that you are mindful of them, human beings that you care for them? You have made them a little lower than the angels and crowned them with glory and honour. You made them rulers over the works of your hands; you put everything under their feet: all flocks and herds, and the animals of the wild, the birds in the sky, and the fish in the sea, all that swim the paths of the seas.*

Just like David all those centuries ago, for most of us it is hard to gaze up at the glittering beauty of the night sky and not think in our heart, 'Somebody did this.' That somebody, our majestic God, has bestowed on you and me the honour and the responsibility to take care of his creation. Among all things, living or technological, it is only humans who are 'crowned with glory and honour'. We alone are stewards. Could AI make us better stewards?

For example, self-driving cars could reduce emissions by 50% by identifying efficient routes and optimising driving speed. AI can analyse massive amounts of data from satellite images to project deforestation or predict coastal communities at risk from flooding. AI is already used to diagnose cancers in humans, as well as diseases in plants and animals. All this benefits both us and 'the flocks and herds… birds in the sky, and the fish in the sea'. There is much to celebrate.

But AI also introduces us to new responsibilities. For example, as technology enables us to live longer, we become subject to 'new illnesses' like Alzheimer's, which previous generations rarely encountered. Are we prepared to help those communities at risk of flooding? Furthermore, AI itself could pose an environmental risk, as the associated computing could generate CO_2 emissions akin to the aviation industry.

AI brings huge opportunities to help care for our world, but with it new responsibilities.

Lord, strengthen my commitment to care for this extraordinary world. As new technologies appear, I pray we have the wisdom and foresight to use them for good. Amen.

Chris Goswami, Baptist Minister, Airport Chaplain and former Tech-Sector Exec

29
EMBODIED

READ HEBREWS 1:2–4 (NRSV)

> *In these last days he has spoken to us by a Son, whom he appointed heir of all things, through whom he also created the worlds. He is the reflection of God's glory and the exact imprint of God's very being, and he sustains all things by his powerful word. When he had made purification for sins, he sat down at the right hand of the Majesty on high, having become as much superior to angels as the name he has inherited is more excellent than theirs.*

This stunning opening to the book of Hebrews tells us that Christ's ministry is vast in scope, yet deeply embodied – from creating and sustaining worlds, to suffering and dying on the cross, and then being raised to sit down in the heights of majesty. In all this, Christ embodies God's glory, showing us who God is. God's glory is not distant and uncaring. Instead, Christ in all his world-shaping power gives himself up to make his people clean.

Because of Christ's purifying work, we can share in his embodied ministry. However, our lives increasingly revolve around routines that lack deep engagement – scrolling on social media, news websites or online shopping apps. Many of these habits depend on AI systems. For example, companies may use AI to highlight attention-grabbing content based on past user behaviour or to monitor and drive workers' productivity.

AI promises instant solutions but tends to keep us glued to our screens, feeling distracted and overwhelmed. We can end up ignoring and demeaning our own embodiment, leading to inaction or even reinforcement of harmful behaviours. These patterns stand in contrast with Christ's self-giving, purifying participation in creation.

AI systems can be extremely useful tools for connecting us to the needs of the world. By prayerfully orienting routines in light of Christ's embodiment of God's glory, we can put AI in its proper place and make room for ourselves and those around us to engage deeply and constructively with God, the world and each other.

Father, may Christ's embodied revelation of you startle us and orient our use of technology for your glory. Amen.

Rachel Siow Robertson, Philosopher, Hong Kong Baptist University

30
THE IMAGE OF GOD

READ GENESIS 1:26–28 (NRSV)

> *So God created humans in his image, in the image of God he created them; male and female he created them. God blessed them, and God said to them, 'Be fruitful and multiply and fill the earth and subdue it and have dominion over the fish of the sea and over the birds of the air and over every living thing that moves upon the earth.'*

vv. 27–28

The Bible tells us that God and people are somehow alike. We are created in God's image. This does not mean that God has a body like ours – as if God has fingers, hair and a liver. Instead, we share in God's character.

One way we share God's character is through our use of language. As we saw yesterday, Hebrews 1:1 reminds us that God has spoken 'in many and various ways'. When we use language, we reveal God's image. We also demonstrate God's likeness in forming relationships. God longs to relate to his people, and we are most fully alive when we relate to one another.

Recent advances in AI have enabled machines to do many of these things. AI can communicate using language. We may even feel as if we have a relationship with a chatbot. So, is AI also in God's image? Not when it comes to language. A toddler may say 'sorry', but not feel remorse or even sound apologetic. It is the same with AI. Although the words may look right, there is no genuine feeling – or even meaning. Relationships are most authentic when we see things from the other person's point of view. This was the point of the incarnation of Jesus. In Christ, God knows the world from the human perspective. A machine will never know what it is to be human. It can never have a real relationship with us.

AI can never show God's image and likeness. Only humans can do that. We are wonderfully and uniquely made.

Creator God, the psalmist reminds us that you have made us little lower than the angels and crowned us with glory and honour. Thank you for the gifts of creativity, language and relationships. Help us to use each one to bring glory to you. Amen.

Tim Bull, Canon at St Albans Cathedral, Software Engineer

31
AI AND GARDENING

READ GENESIS 2:15 (NIV)

> *The Lord God took the man and put him in the Garden of Eden to work it and take care of it.*

Regardless of our job or role in society, we are all, at our core, gardeners – cultivators of the world. I am not much of a literal gardener myself, but I know that gardening consists of fulfilling two equally important tasks: releasing potential and maintaining the conditions of flourishing.

Our core purpose is to 'work' the garden of the world, releasing its abundant potential for all to enjoy. Alas, extraction and exploitation have been a dominant story in our world. We are equally called to 'take care of' the garden, fostering the conditions of flourishing and fruitfulness with reverent care.

Throughout history, humans have crafted tools. From spears and ploughs to steam engines and computers, tools have increased human force and capability. We have used them both to work and to exploit the garden of the world, to nurture and to undermine the conditions of flourishing.

With the arrival of increasingly capable AI systems and other so-called frontier technologies, our fundamental purpose remains the same. As in the past, we can release potential and nurture 'the life of the world', rather than exploit our neighbours and extract from creation. Yet the challenge is steeper because of the unprecedented power of our latest tools.

How might you use a powerful AI assistant to bless others and bring out the best of them? If you are, say, a teacher, you might use AI to help craft an engaging lesson that will stretch and delight your pupils. If you work in the corporate sector, an AI assistant might help finally organise your life and release precious time to give to your church community, family and friends.

Father God, please help me to discern what I can do to help ensure that AI and other cutting-edge tools are used to release rather than extract potential, to nurture rather than destroy the conditions of flourishing for all your creatures. Amen.

Nathan Mladin, Theologian, Theos

32
FALLEN

READ GENESIS 3:6–8 (NIV)

> When the woman saw that the fruit of the tree was good for food and pleasing to the eye, and also desirable for gaining wisdom, she took some and ate it. She also gave some to her husband, who was with her, and he ate it. Then the eyes of both of them were opened, and they realised they were naked; so they sewed fig leaves together and made coverings for themselves. Then the man and his wife heard the sound of the Lord God as he was walking in the garden in the cool of the day, and they hid from the Lord God among the trees of the garden.

AI systems are tools, and like any other tools humankind has crafted, they can work for or against us. AI tools created by organisations and governments will not be perfect, as we ourselves are imperfect fallen beings.

AI tools are powerful: the organisations behind them have the potential to know a lot about us, to be ubiquitous, as AIs are increasingly 'present' in multiple kinds of devices, and to make decisions about us or on our behalf. AI systems have been empowered by humans (and their data) to recommend, predict, select and decide. As access to these tools are not equitably distributed, they have the potential to divide humanity into 'the haves' and 'the have nots' digitally, socially, even politically, and physically. This means AI can discriminate based on existing human biases and further entrench existing systemic societal inequalities.

God's position has not changed. God is still omniscient, omnipresent and omnipotent. So when God says, 'Do not fear, for I am with you' (Isaiah 41:10), 'Do not conform to the pattern of this world, but be transformed by the renewing of your mind' (Romans 12:2) and 'Seek justice. Defend the oppressed' (Isaiah 1:17), he means it!

Father, help us to not fear AI or the power that it could wield. Give us your wisdom and discernment as to when, how and why we use AI tools. Use our ability to think critically and to challenge what we see, including decisions about people that are made autonomously or augmented using artificial intelligence. Amen.

Patricia Shaw, Founder of Beyond Reach Consulting, Lawyer, AI and Data Ethics Consultant

33
WORK AND REST

READ GENESIS 2:2–3 (NRSV)

> *On the sixth day God finished the work that he had done, and he rested on the seventh day from all the work that he had done. So God blessed the seventh day and hallowed it, because on it God rested from all the work that he had done in creation.*

When Michael Schluter set up the secular Keep Sunday Special campaign in 1985, it was widely believed that all-week trading would damage families, communities and local economies. Meanwhile the Lord's Day Observance Society (now known as Day One Christian Ministries) campaigned for no Sunday working on the Christian sabbath – the day of rest. The Jewish sabbath is Saturday – the last day of the week – and the fourth commandment relates to it (Exodus 20:8). The biblical rationale makes sense of the secular need for restful time and the secular argument chimes with the biblical imperative. Yet we now live in a seven-day-a-week, 24/7 world.

Why did God rest on the seventh day? For humanity, rest is about stopping and stepping out of the routine, just sleeping sometimes. Whether it is physical, mental or pastoral labour, well-being requires a break from it. Yet God's rest is also about contemplation: to comprehend and appreciate. One can be so engrossed in work that there is no rest for reflection. Unable to reflect from within the task, one needs to pause and survey. This is purposeful rest. St Benedict called prayer the 'work of God', but prayer is simultaneously, paradoxically perhaps, a form of rest too.

If AI is going to ease workloads and give us more time, the godly purpose of that time is something which many people increasingly say they have no time for: prayer. AI gives an opportunity to rest in the Lord and work at prayer. The time AI will save is a gift for some. God built time for restful reflection into the created order. AI may yet release and enhance that gracious gift by which we can contemplate faith and life and, through prayer, build on our relationship with God, Father, Son and Holy Spirit.

God, help us always to take time to rest in you and truly appreciate your wonderful work as creator, redeemer and sustainer. Amen.

Gordon Giles, Church of England Canon, Musician and Philosopher

Opposite: nerve cells (neurons in the brain)

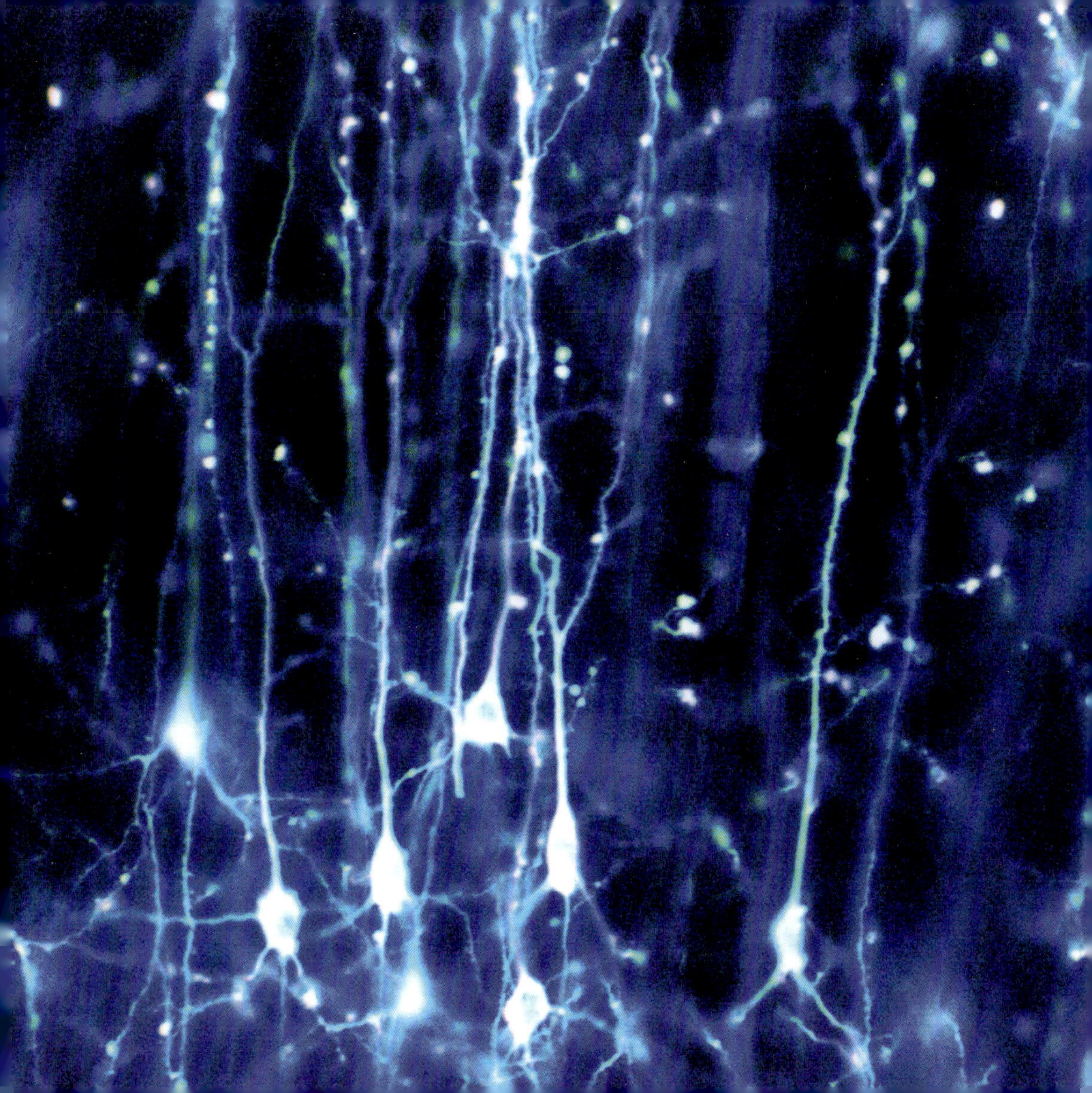

34
IDOLATRY

READ ISAIAH 44:9–20 (NRSV)

> *The carpenter… plants a cedar and the rain nourishes it… Half of it he burns in the fire; over this half he roasts meat, eats it, and is satisfied… The rest of it he makes into a god, his idol, bows down to it, and worships it.*

vv. 13–14, 16–17

I am certain artificial intelligence will be as revolutionary as the microscope. As a neuroscientist and consultant neurologist, I see the potential for AI to analyse vast amounts of data in a way that was impossible ten years ago, or to improve the diagnostic accuracy of scans by limiting human error. However, we must not be dazzled by its potential and must always retain a sense of perspective. Yes, it can process data at vast speeds, but AI will never have the empathy, understanding and humanity of a scientist or clinician.

Idols from scripture may seem very remote from our own experience, but it is worth remembering that idols were objects that were created by a people seeking an alternative to God's gifts and blessings. They became blinded by the craftsman's skill, placing their trust in these objects rather than God.

AI is a tool that we can (and should) use positively, but when we see AI as a 'better' alternative to the skills and empathy of humanity, whether it is in healthcare or science, we are at risk of placing our faith in this man-made tool and celebrating it above God's creation. If we do this, we too become guilty of the idolatry described in scripture, using microchips and computer code rather than wood like the carpenter in Isaiah.

We can be thankful for AI and the change it will bring to our lives, but we must also remember that it will never surpass the beauty and wonder of God's creation. If we suggest otherwise, we risk creating a new idol for our modern world and forgetting the warning of Isaiah, which still resonates strongly today.

Lord, grant us the grace to celebrate the developments in science that you have gifted to us and the humility to recognise these tools are nothing compared to the beauty and wonder of your creation. Amen.

The Revd Professor Ian Morrison, Consultant Neurologist and Church of Scotland Minister

35
BEGOTTEN

READ GENESIS 5:1–3 (NIV)

> *When God created mankind, he made them in the likeness of God. He created them male and female and blessed them. And he named them 'Mankind' when they were created. When Adam had lived 130 years, he had a son in his own likeness, in his own image; and he named him Seth.*

The Bible teaches that human beings are created in God's image. So some people have suggested that when we humans invent AI machines, we are somehow creating new beings in our own image. But our passage shows that Adam passes on the mysterious image and likeness of God, not in what he makes, but in the child that he fathers. The Hebrew word *yalad*, rendered by the NIV as 'had a son', is translated in the Authorised Version with the old English word 'begot'. Just as the Son was 'begotten not made' (in the words of the Nicene Creed), so in biblical thinking the same applies to our biological children. They also are 'begotten not made'. We pass on the image of God to the children we beget.

When we make something it is a product of our will, it is different from us and it is ours to control. But when we beget a child, this new and wonderful being is not a product of our will, but a gift from our nature. He or she is fundamentally the same as us, and, as every parent learns, we are not able to control and direct our children. We must set them free to be themselves. So, however sophisticated and powerful AI machines may become, we must always remember that they are designed and produced by human beings; they are a product of human choices and intentions. Machines are not free to follow their own path. A healthy relationship with AI depends on understanding that humans define what AI means and what role it should play in society. When used with wisdom, AI can help us to flourish, but it can never replace us.

Father, thank you that your precious image is passed on to the next generation as we beget children. Teach us to develop a healthy relationship with AI that helps us to flourish and become the people you meant us to be. Amen.

John Wyatt, Neonatologist and Ethicist

36
MANNERS MATTER

READ PROVERBS 12:10 (NRSV)

> *The righteous know the needs of their animals, but the mercy of the wicked is cruel.*

'Manners maketh man.' The politeness, respect and courtesy which make up good manners are essential to humanity in the building and restoring of relationships. The character of a person is determined not only by the attitude they have but also by how they treat people and things that they deem lesser or weaker than them. So does it matter how we treat an AI machine? Proverbs 12:10 makes reference to humans and animals, both of which were created in service to God, and the stewardship responsibility of humanity is to respect and care for God's creation. How we treat animals matters, and how we relate to each other is equally important. There is need for compassionate consideration and kindness by adopting a way of thinking and doing that evidences our practical and moral responsibility. Sadly, the attitude of the wicked is described as cruel – lacking any sense of gentleness, kindness or consideration to things, let alone people.

In a world with created technology advancing exponentially, AI-powered systems are not only influencing the way we live or think, but in some aspects they reflect our attitudes and behaviour. While chatbot technology, such as ChatGPT, or virtual assistants, like Alexa, Cortana, Bixby, Siri and Google Assistant, are not able to process human emotions at the moment, they use AI algorithms for speech recognition, to understand language processing, answering questions quicker than humans can through expert systems, performing tasks like setting reminders, playing our favourite music or providing us direction using polite and courteous voice tones.

Is it possible that when we are harsh, rude and impatient with virtual assistants, these tendencies creep in to how we treat or communicate with others? How are these observed behaviours teaching children to be polite and considerate to others, including AI-powered systems?

Lord, make me an instrument of kindness, being compassionate and well-mannered with all I meet, in all I say and all I do. Amen.

Charmaine Mhlanga, Baptist Minister and former Care Home Manager

37
CREATIVITY

READ EXODUS 31:1–6 (NRSV)

> *The Lord spoke to Moses, 'See, I have called by name Bezalel son of Uri son of Hur, of the tribe of Judah, and I have filled him with a divine spirit, with ability, intelligence, and knowledge, and every kind of skill, to devise artistic designs, to work in gold, silver, and bronze, in cutting stones for setting, and in carving wood, to work in every kind of craft. Moreover, I have appointed with him Oholiab son of Ahisamach, of the tribe of Dan, and I have given skill to all the skilful, so that they may make all that I have commanded you.*

Machines have already 'turned their hands' to a variety of art forms. Computer-generated poetry has been around for decades. Algorithms are regularly used to compose new music. In 2022 the humanoid robot, Ai-Da, painted a portrait of the late Queen Elizabeth II.

Bezalel and Oholiab received God-given gifts of human creativity. Through the power of the Holy Spirit, they became skilled artists. They were commissioned to put their gifts to work in the service of God, at the time when a tabernacle was being constructed in his name.

As machines become increasingly able to mimic human creativity, we face a choice. We can yield that ground to manufactured devices. We surrender the realms of poetry, conversation, painting and music. We retreat into ever smaller arenas in which to express talents which machines cannot yet mimic.

Or we choose a different route. We decide that whatever creativity may be mimicked, we have a God-given call to be creative. The Holy Spirit invites us to know his empowering as we seek to flourish as the creative beings God calls us to become.

We all have different perspectives on our own creative abilities, and on whether or not we view AI as a tool to enhance those gifts. Whatever those perspectives, we are all made in God's image, and so all designed to be creative in turn. We are all called to use that creativity in his service.

Lord, we thank you for your awesome gifts of creativity within us. Give us wisdom that we may release those gifts for your glory. In Jesus' name. Amen.

Justin Tomkins, Church of England Priest and Scientist

38
COMFORTING WORDS

READ PSALM 147:1–11 (NIV)

> *Praise the Lord. How good it is to sing praises to our God, how pleasant and fitting to praise him!… He heals the broken-hearted and binds up their wounds. He determines the number of the stars and calls them each by name. Great is our Lord and mighty in power; his understanding has no limit. The Lord sustains the humble but casts the wicked to the ground. Sing to the Lord with grateful praise; make music to our God on the harp.*

vv. 1, 3–7

One of the earliest uses of AI was in cognitive behavioural therapy, which has been shown to be effective in the treatment of anxiety, depression and a range of other issues. Problematic behaviours are 'challenged' using exercises, experiments and so on, with the goal of learning about the relationship with harmful thoughts and behaviours and ultimately reducing their occurrence. Therapists quickly realised that aspects of this process could be automated, using simple forms of AI to generate questions, responses and challenges.

Should we as Christians put our faith in AI in this way? While we value the skills and abilities of professionally trained counsellors, for many of us our first recourse when facing challenging times and situations may be to seek solace and advice from trusted friends or pastors. We may be advised to seek additional help from professionals (AI-augmented or otherwise) where appropriate. We also know, in our hearts, that God is the one to whom we can turn at any time.

However well trained, AI – like humans – will sometimes fall short. Scripture often reminds us, as in this psalm, of both the great gentleness and yet awesome power of the Lord. God is the one who never fails. The one who is able to carefully bind our wounds when we need to be cared for is also the awesome one, who knows the names of all the stars in the universe.

Infinitely wise as well as being endlessly caring, God is the only one whose understanding is limitless.

We give thanks for the health many of us enjoy. Thank you for the benefits which science and technology bring in keeping us healthy. Amen.

Murdo Macdonald, Policy Officer, Church of Scotland Society, Religion and Technology

39
PROTECTORS

READ GENESIS 9:5–6 (NIV)

> *'And for your lifeblood I will surely demand an accounting. I will demand an accounting from every animal. And from each human being, too, I will demand an accounting for the life of another human being. Whoever sheds human blood, by humans shall their blood be shed; for in the image of God has God made mankind.'*

Genesis 9 describes God's re-creation of the world. The creation was 'very good' (Genesis 1:31), but that did not last. Sin had taken hold, leading to murder (Genesis 3—4). The wickedness became so great that God resolved to put an end to all people (Genesis 6). We then come to the aftermath of the flood and God's second creation.

There are many echoes of the first creation – separating dry land from water, the reappearance of plants, the repopulation of the world with animals, a command for

Noah and his sons to be fruitful and increase in number. But there is a difference. God has to spell out the value of human life and the punishment for murder. God has made us in his image; human life is very precious and to be treated with respect.

God still permits shedding blood, not least as Joshua led the Israelites into the promised land. There are times when we still need armed forces and when taking human life is the lesser of two evils, but we will be held to account. These are not decisions to be delegated casually to automated systems. Autonomous weapons that identify hostile targets and eliminate them without human intervention are very attractive to the military and law-enforcement agencies. Very cost-effective as they are, God will demand an accounting for the life of another human from their operators.

Blood is precious to God in this re-creation. The rainbow calls us to peace while reminding us of God's love, love ultimately fulfilled in the blood of Jesus on the cross that guarantees our place in the new creation that is to come.

Lord God, thank you for making us in your image. Please help us to respect that image faithfully and responsibly in a fallen world. Amen.

Peter Robinson, Emeritus Professor of Computer Technology, and President of Gonville and Caius College, University of Cambridge

40
INCARNATED TEACHING

READ MATTHEW 28:19–20 (NIV)

> *'Therefore go and make disciples of all nations, baptising them in the name of the Father and of the Son and of the Holy Spirit, and teaching them to obey everything I have commanded you. And surely I am with you always, to the very end of the age.'*

Modern technology is amazing. Google can tell you almost anything you want to know. Whatever question my kids have, ChatGPT can tell them an answer in less time than it takes me to look up from my cup of tea and ask them to repeat themselves. If technology puts all possible information in the palm of your hand, what do we – mere human beings – have to offer the next generation, or any generation? Much in every way!

Jesus' instruction to his disciples is not to *tell* people, so that they know information. Rather, it is to *teach* people, so that they obey his commands. Jesus commands us, for example, to love one another. The simplest AI can tell a person to obey Jesus' command to love; it takes only a few words. But what does it take to teach someone to obey Jesus' command to love? It takes a life that shows that it is possible, day after day, year after year, to be kind, gracious, forgiving, patient, self-controlled and hopeful. Not simply *saying* that it is possible, but *showing* that it is possible.

It may take being awake at 3.00 am, holding a person's hand as we identify with their suffering, weeping bitterly with them, sharing silent recognition that words will not do and that none of the nice, neat answers make any sense. Teaching to love requires showing that in real, messy life, you love. And you continue to love even when you stand to lose everything you hold dear, because that is how obedience to the command works.

God places great significance in humans. We are divinely called to a task that cannot be accomplished by anything else. We can let technology tell. But we must not think that this does away with our task to teach.

God, thank you for the place that you have given to humanity in your plan for building your kingdom. Amen.

Mike Brownnutt, Philosopher of Science and Religion, and Course Director, The Faraday Institute for Science and Religion

41
INCREASINGLY HUMAN

READ 2 CORINTHIANS 3:17–18 (NRSV)

> *Now the Lord is the Spirit, and where the Spirit of the Lord is, there is freedom. And all of us, with unveiled faces, seeing the glory of the Lord as though reflected in a mirror, are being transformed into the same image from one degree of glory to another; for this comes from the Lord, the Spirit.*

AI is humanity's most powerful tool, the first in history that seems able to make decisions and create new ideas by itself. The latest chatbots' responses are so human-like, it is easy to feel confused about the nature of our relationship with AI. But while amazingly capable and clever, AI chatbots are really only simulating a human response, predicting the most probable next word based on having absorbed vast quantities of human writing and online content. AI is but a pale reflection of humanity when compared against the eternal 'glory of the Lord' in whose image we are beautifully and wonderfully made.

Today's passage reminds us of our freedom in Christ – freedom to be allowed into the presence of God and freedom to be transformed ever more deeply into his likeness by his Spirit. Unlike an AI, we have been given by God the ability to love, to enjoy deep relationship with him and our fellow humans, to be self-aware and to be able to contemplate our place in his universe. It is in relationship with God and our fellow humans that we find true meaning and value, not in pseudo-relationships with AI entities which reflect back our own desires and leave us open to manipulation.

It is important to be informed about AI, the great opportunities for society and the risks of harm, and to be comfortable to engage with technology as a tool to serve and help humanity. But we can also encourage one another that relationship fulfilment is found in our freedom to love and worship God, who knows and cares for us deeply, and in the gift of loving relationships with other humans made in his image.

Thank you, Lord, that I am intimately known and loved by you and am being continuously transformed into your likeness through the saving grace of Christ. Help me to engage with technology in a healthy way. Amen.

Graham Budd, Executive Director, The Faraday Institute for Science and Religion

PART VI

CARING FOR CREATION

The BBC television series *Wild Isles* (2023) was a vivid reminder not just of how beautiful the UK is in the diversity and richness of its wildlife, but how ravaged it has been by climate change, pollution, poor land management, unsustainable fishing practices and habitat destruction. Sir David Attenborough reminded the viewer at regular intervals that, with under 50% of our biodiversity left, the UK is in the bottom 10% of countries worldwide for conservation.

The biblical story is a vivid retelling of this dynamic: of humankind having been called to care for creation but instead acting out of selfishness to cause destruction. There is a call to lament, but not despair. These reflections take the reader through that drama, from the wonder and beauty of creation, through ruination and grief,

Opposite: cumulus clouds with crepuscular rays

to strength for today and hope for the future. To complete our 52 devotions, we will take you deeper into a set of passages from both Old and New Testaments, including some that are often used in the context of this topic and others that are not.

The contributors in this section include representatives from The John Ray Initiative, A Rocha and Tearfund. Our ultimate aim is to link the latest science with up-to-date theology and biblical scholarship, helping you navigate this important and at times difficult field. Our hope is that we will challenge and inspire you in your journey of creation care.

Ruth M. Bancewicz

42
TILL AND KEEP

READ GENESIS 1:24–31; 2:7–17 (NRSV)

> *Then God said, 'Let us make humans in our image, according to our likeness, and let them have dominion over the fish of the sea and over the birds of the air and over the cattle and over all the wild animals of the earth and over every creeping thing that creeps upon the earth.' So God created humans in his image, in the image of God he created them; male and female he created them… Then the Lord God formed man from the dust of the ground and breathed into his nostrils the breath of life, and the man became a living being. And the Lord God planted a garden in Eden, in the east, and there he put the man whom he had formed.*

vv. 1:26–27; 2:7–8

No part of the Bible has generated more contested interpretation than Genesis 1—3. The twin accounts of creation (1:1–2:4a and 2:4b–25) and the entrance of sin into God's good creation (3:1–24) touch on issues including cosmic origins, human nature, gender and sexuality, good and evil, divine purpose and the nature of biblical literature. Here we will limit ourselves to the question, 'What are humans for?', the issue of biblical anthropology.

The phrase 'image of God' (1:26–27) appears in the Hebrew Bible only here and briefly in Genesis 5:1–3 and 9:6. Despite its absence in the rest of the Old Testament, it has been a hugely influential phrase. Arguably, it has inspired the secular concept of human rights, whereby all people, regardless of difference, are of equal value. There have been three broad theological interpretations concerning 'image of God' in humanity: *substantive* (a unique God-given capacity, such as reason, will or conscience), *relational* (the human capacity for relationship with God) and *functional* (a task God gives to humanity). Today, most biblical scholars take the functional view, based on parallels from other ancient Near Eastern religions and the actual context of Genesis 1, where 'image of God' is related to the task of having 'dominion' over the earth and its creatures. To put it simply, bearing God's image is a job description involving delegated responsibility to reflect God's intentions towards creation.

Genesis 2:7 gives a very different, but complementary, perspective on what it means to be human. Rather than exalted as the image of God, humans (*Adam*) are formed from the dust of the ground (*Adamah*). Biologically, this is obvious. We are carbon-based life-forms related to all other earth creatures. Theologically, this is crucial too. We cannot separate ourselves from nature. We are called to reflect God's image among, not above, our fellow creatures.

That brings us to 2:15–17, where God places the first human in the garden to 'till it and keep it'. The words 'till' and 'keep' cover both agricultural cultivation and the priestly task of serving and guarding in God's temple. This, in essence, is our job description, our first great commission. Creation is a temple to God's glory and we are placed within it to reflect God's image on behalf of our fellow creatures. We glorify God by enabling the flourishing and fruitfulness of God's earth. That, in Genesis 1—2, is what humans are for!

Creator God, teach us to act with humility and wisdom as we bear your image in caring for our fellow creatures.

Dave Bookless, Head of Theology, A Rocha International

43

BROKEN RELATIONSHIPS

READ GENESIS 3:16–24; 4:1–16 (NRSV)

> *To the woman he said, 'I will make your pangs in childbirth exceedingly great; in pain you shall bring forth children, yet your desire shall be for your husband, and he shall rule over you.' And to the man he said, 'Because you have listened to the voice of your wife and have eaten of the tree about which I commanded you, "You shall not eat of it", cursed is the ground because of you; in toil you shall eat of it all the days of your life… And the Lord said, 'What have you done? Listen, your brother's blood is crying out to me from the ground! And now you are cursed from the ground, which has opened its mouth to receive your brother's blood from your hand… And the Lord put a mark on Cain, so that no one who came upon him would kill him.*

vv. 3:16–17; 4:10–11, 15

When Adam and Eve rebelled against God by disobeying him, they set the pattern for all humanity. The consequences were immediate. The breakdown of harmonious relations between humans and God spread to alienation from the created order. This in turn led to disruption in interpersonal relationships, culminating in the first murder recorded in the Bible. Although the general consequences of sin for both Adam and Eve were similar, God pronounced sentences specific to each.

The woman's 'wages of sin' relate to her roles as mother and wife (3:16). Her pains in childbirth were exacerbated. Despite the suffering involved, humans retained the blessing and power of procreation God had given them. But as with all sin, the good that God had brought forth was marred. Sin caused Eve's relationship to Adam to be disrupted, bringing male tyranny and domination into what had been a loving partnership.

For the man, the consequences of putting himself first instead of God were that his relationship to the very ground from which his crops came was cursed. Instead of joyful work in the garden, it became painful toil and a struggle to produce food (3:17–19). The change was not in the nature of the earth and plants themselves, but in the insatiable greed and self-centredness of humans, which pollutes and destroys the earth on which we depend. As we see clearly with climate change and the unprecedented (in human history) rate of species extinctions, we are quite literally turning a garden into a desert.

Lastly, Cain murdered his younger brother Abel. Abel had pleased God by sacrificing the firstborn of his flocks (4:4). Cain had brought some of his crops (4:3), but God wasn't pleased with that. We are not told why; maybe Cain didn't give sacrificially. But it made Cain angry enough to kill, despite God trying to reason with him (4:5–8). Cain's real motive seems to be that he thought he could buy God's favour, and he could not bear the idea of the sovereign God choosing to recognise his brother's faith. Cain was thrown out of his home and family, but even in his wandering God showed mercy by preventing anyone killing him (4:13–15). Likewise, God shows us mercy in our sinfulness, culminating in the sacrifice of his own Son to restore us to relationship with himself.

Father God, thank you that through Jesus' death on the cross we can now be restored to relationship with you. Thank you that in the new creation all relationships between creator, creation and us your creatures will be fully restored without any trace of sin or death. Amen

Robert White, Emeritus Director, The Faraday Institute for Science and Religion, and Emeritus Professor of Geophysics, University of Cambridge

44
BROKEN WORLD

READ ISAIAH 24:1–3, 10–23 (NRSV)

> *Now the Lord is about to lay waste the earth and make it desolate, and he will twist its surface and scatter its inhabitants… The city of chaos is broken down; every house is shut up so that no one can enter. There is an outcry in the streets for lack of wine; all joy has reached its eventide; the gladness of the earth is banished. Desolation is left in the city; the gates are battered into ruins. For thus it shall be on the earth and among the nations, as when an olive tree is beaten, as at the gleaning when the grape harvest is ended.*

vv. 1, 10–13

With a cluster of vivid poetic images, Isaiah 24 laments the groaning of the earth under the weight of cosmic evil. The Hebrew people never thought of the world as an autonomous, self-sustaining life system ('nature') but, rather, as a *creation* dependent moment by moment on the faithfulness of Yahweh, its creator. Human wickedness, springing from the rejection of Yahweh's moral norms and the Adamic covenant, devastates the planet and destroys social life (vv. 10–13), since human well-being and the integrity of the fragile ecological system of the food chain are intimately connected. The fecundity of the earth is disrupted. It is as if the ordered creation itself is being undone, returning to the primeval chaos (v. 10).

This could be read easily as a litany of environmental ills culled from our daily news media: military conflicts that scorch the earth; the large-scale plundering of natural resources; the destruction of ecosystems that lead to the rapid extinction of fauna and flora; uncontrolled greenhouse emissions that intensify droughts and floods and wreak havoc on weather patterns.

In a move typical of prophetic imagination, Isaiah sees such human-induced planetary chaos as a harbinger of Yahweh's own approaching judgement. Yahweh has an appointed day when he will punish the kings of the earth and the cosmic powers that uphold an idolatrous world system (v. 21). The earth will be 'laid waste', made utterly desolate (vv. 1, 3). All alike will suffer, irrespective of social position or function (v. 2). Such indiscriminate judgement raises awkward questions, then and now. Why does the oppressed suffer along with the oppressor? It seems that we, as a result of our social nature, are 'all in it together'.

However, when the world system is judged, those who have no stake in its perpetuation will rejoice and give praise to Yahweh (vv. 14–16a). We are not told who 'they' are, but they are clearly the faithful community of Yahweh who await his intervention. They come not from the centres of political and economic power, but from all over the world, including the remote 'coastlands of the sea' (v. 15). For them, the judgement on a cruel and exploitative world order is good news. It paves the way for a new regime of global governance under Yahweh (v. 23), the dawn of a renewed creation.

Father, we grieve at the indifference of governments to the devastation of your earth. We long for you to judge them and free the earth from their rapacious rule.

Vinoth Ramachandra, former Secretary for Dialogue and Social Engagement, International Fellowship of Evangelical Students

45

THE EARTH MOURNS

READ ISAIAH 24:4–10 (ESV)

> *The earth mourns and withers; the world languishes and withers; the highest people of the earth languish… The wine mourns, the vine languishes, all the merry-hearted sigh. The mirth of the tambourines is stilled, the noise of the jubilant has ceased, the mirth of the lyre is stilled. No more do they drink wine with singing; strong drink is bitter to those who drink it. The wasted city is broken down; every house is shut up so that none can enter.*

vv. 4, 7–10

Recently, I interviewed two botanical scientists at Kew Gardens. One is a Christian and the other avowedly not, yet they both expressed the same response to the conclusions of their research: lament. One shared with me that while working in the Brazilian Atlantic Forest, one of the richest ecosystems in the world, she found that just a single teaspoonful of soil contained around 1,800 plant species – the same number as we have in the whole of the UK. The other shared his experience with the ash dieback pandemic, a disease that is devastating the world's ash trees. The cause? Human irresponsibility in transporting trees carrying pests into gardens around the world.

The interaction between humans and the natural environment ('the earth') is a serious one when viewed from the perspective of God's holiness and human irresponsibility. Such appalling creation abuse should break our hearts like it did Isaiah's, like it does God's, and, in anthropomorphic terms, like it does the 'earth' (v. 4). Surely there can be only one appropriate response: lament, repentance and trust in the same Saviour the whole of creation is looking for with outstretched neck to bring redemption at the last (Romans 8:19–23).

Isaiah says the earth 'mourns' (v. 4) – it is languishing, not flourishing, a lamentable shadow of what it was created to be. In fact, 'the earth lies defiled' (v. 5). But who is *responsible* for this defilement? Not the creator, but the whole of 'earth's inhabitants' are responsible (vv. 5–6). By flouting the principles of the earth's care, those charged with that task have in fact abused it. Today, we speak of the raping of the earth. This passage is a vivid description of the horrific abuse carried out upon creation by its human carers. As the following verses make clear, such creation abuse will inevitably make lives miserable and empty (v.v. 6–9) as the 'earth' is left lying in misery and shame, as if 'cursed.' But the reality is that the 'earth' is innocent; it is her shameless carers who have committed the horrendous evil. This is why the attitude and practice of lament are the only appropriate stances we humans should adopt, all the more so as the ravages of human-induced climate change are accelerating misery in a mourning earth.

With broken hearts we lament to you our vandalism of your beautiful creation. We throw ourselves on your mercy and grace for forgiveness and help.

Roger Abbott, Pastor and Practical Theologian

46
GOD'S COMMITMENT

READ GENESIS 9:1–17 (NRSV)

> *The fear and dread of you shall rest on every animal of the earth and on every bird of the air, on everything that creeps on the ground and on all the fish of the sea; into your hand they are delivered. Every moving thing that lives shall be food for you, and just as I gave you the green plants, I give you everything. Only, you shall not eat flesh with its life, that is, its blood… Then God said to Noah and to his sons with him, 'As for me, I am establishing my covenant with you and your descendants after you and with every living creature that is with you, the birds, the domestic animals, and every animal of the earth with you, as many as came out of the ark. I establish my covenant with you, that never again shall all flesh be cut off by the waters of a flood, and never again shall there be a flood to destroy the earth.'*

vv. 2–4, 8–11

In 2022 the UK parliament passed the Animal Welfare (Sentience) Act. This acknowledged that animals experience emotions and feel pain. Moreover, it goes beyond vertebrates, and animals such as lobsters and octopuses now have some welfare protection for the first time. Paradoxically, the law does not outlaw existing practices, so lobsters can still be boiled alive, despite evidence that they experience pain and distress.

Genesis begins by portraying a harmonious relationship between humans and animals, but the breakdown in relationships resulting from the fall in Genesis 3 leaves animals vulnerable to human ill-treatment. By the time of Noah, animals have become fearful of humans. The flood brings a fresh start, and God resets the relationships between humans and the rest of his creation. God sets limits. Humans are now allowed to eat animals but must slaughter them, draining out the life-giving blood. Ancient Hebrews believed that the soul (*nephesh*) resided in the blood of a creature. Since it was breathed into them by God, it should be drained back to the ground and not consumed. Furthermore, God would demand a reckoning for not keeping this commandment and for shedding human blood.

The covenant with Noah is a universal covenant made between God, humans and animals. It is interesting that, when the early Jewish Christians wrote to the new Gentile believers (Acts 15), they quoted from this covenant. Gentiles had never been required to follow Mosaic laws, but these Noachian laws were seen as universal.

Alongside these limits, God places a limit on himself. When the rainbow appears, he will remember the covenant. So this covenant is making the best of circumstances that are not ideal. The world is no longer perfect, but God loves his creation and wants us to partner with him in its care. God blesses Noah and encourages him to be fruitful and multiply. The word 'fill' (*mala*) could also mean 'replenish'. This repeats the command in Genesis 1:28, but omits the command to 'subdue'. Maybe humans had wrongly taken that command as freedom to damage and destroy? Today, the protection of the biodiversity of this planet is in our hands. Let us work with God and be guided by him in our care for creation, to replenish and not harm.

Lord, it grieves us to see the suffering of creatures you have made and love. Help us to care for animals alongside humans and bless our efforts with the harmony only you can bring.

Margot Hodson, Director of Theology and Education, The John Ray Initiative

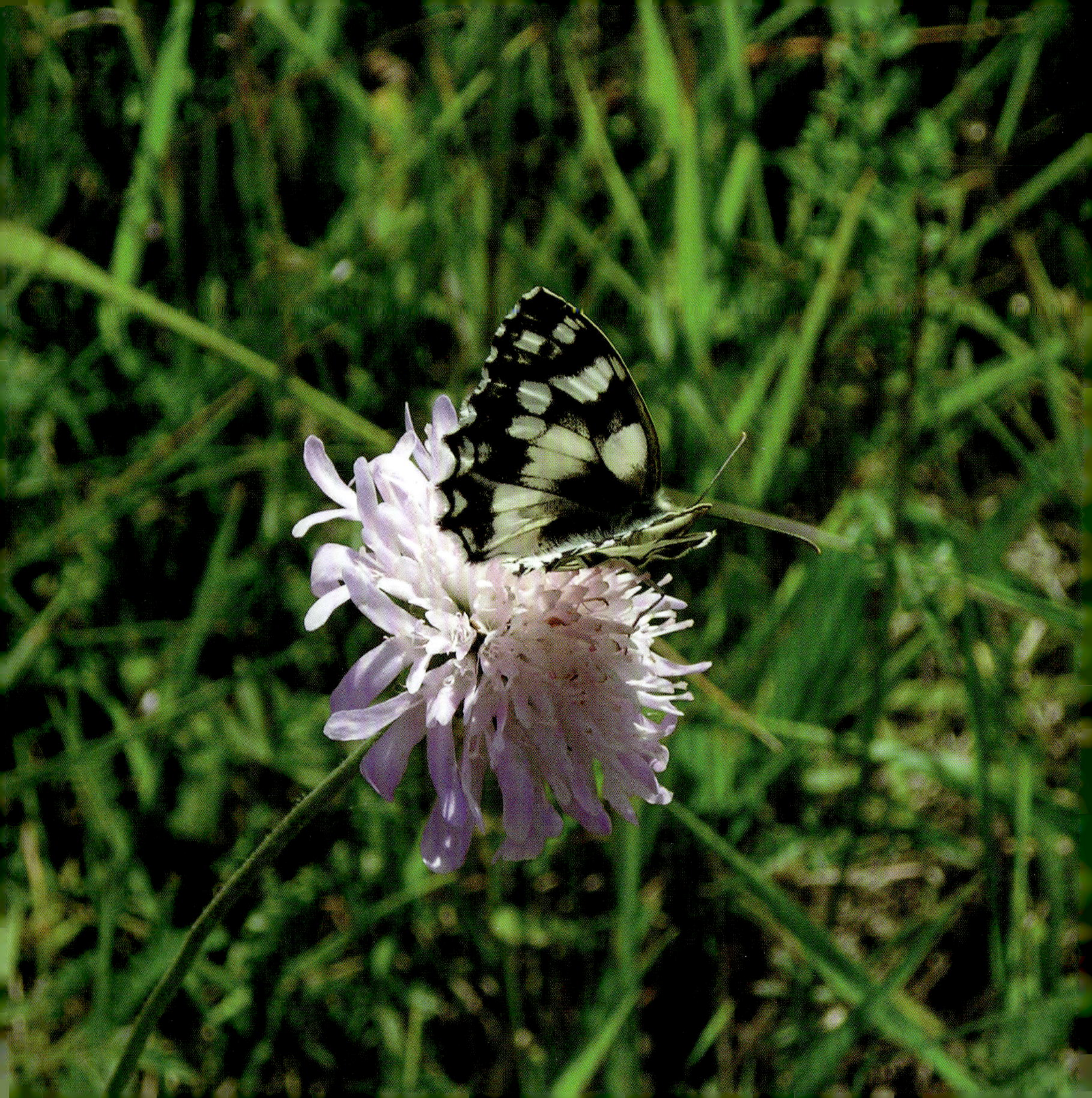

47
CREATION IS STILL GOOD

READ PSALM 8 (NRSV)

> *O Lord, our Sovereign, how majestic is your name in all the earth!*

v. 1

As a scientist I have been privileged to have seen and discovered some things that nobody else ever saw or knew about before. For many years, I used electron microscopes to look at plant cells and tissues at very high magnification. I really was seeing some of the work of God's fingers, and I still feel amazingly blessed to have had those opportunities. If I was looking at the micro-scale, then Psalm 8 definitely begins at the macro-scale. While I was investigating plant ultrastructure, the psalm first considers the heavens, the stars and the moon, before moving on to mammals, birds and fish.

Psalm 8 is short, but expansive, taking in the whole created order. David's psalm is a song of praise bookended by 'O Lord, our Sovereign, how majestic is your name in all

Opposite: a Marbled White butterfly (Melanargia galathea)

the earth!' It is clearly related to the creation narratives in Genesis 1 and 2, in which creation is seen as 'good'. But as we know, Genesis 3 soon follows, where human sin causes the damaging of relationships between God, humans and the environment.

Throughout history some have thought that the fall so corrupted the earth that it became evil. This has led people to believe that the only way out from this degraded world is to escape to some sort of perfect higher spiritual realm. This kind of dualistic thinking, which still exists in some parts of the church today, has been very harmful. If the creation is evil, there is no point in caring for it. If all our focus is on attaining a higher spiritual existence, then we will hardly show any concern for the environment.

But look again at Psalm 8. There is no indication at all that the created order is bad or evil. This psalm was written well after the fall, and David would have been well aware of Genesis 3. In fact, if we take the whole Bible into account there is no sign that the creation itself is bad. Other psalms confirm this. For instance, Psalm 24:1 has: 'The earth is the Lord's and all that is in it, the world, and those who live in it.' It may be marred by human sin, but the creation still belongs to God and is basically good – at both the micro- and macro-scales!

Lord, we thank you for the goodness of your creation, and pray that all parts of your church will come to realise this is the case. Amen.

Martin Hodson, Principal Tutor of Christian Rural and Environmental Studies, The John Ray Initiative

48
SUSTAINER

READ PSALM 147 (NRSV)

> *Praise the Lord! How good it is to sing praises to our God, for he is gracious, and a song of praise is fitting… He determines the number of the stars; he gives to all of them their names. Great is our Lord and abundant in power; his understanding is beyond measure… He covers the heavens with clouds, prepares rain for the earth, makes grass grow on the hills. He gives to the animals their food and to the young ravens when they cry… He sends out his command to the earth; his word runs swiftly. He gives snow like wool; he scatters frost like ashes.*

vv. 1, 4–5, 8–9, 15–16

Psalm 147 is a song of praise to God for his provision and power, probably written when the Israelites returned to Jerusalem following their exile in Babylon. It contains jubilant stanzas of celebration that God has provided security and peace for his people, who had been through tough times (vv. 2–3), and abundant provision for their physical needs in their own land (v. 14). It is a resounding affirmation that Yahweh, not the gods of Babylon, is sovereign over everything. The God of Zion orchestrates the weather to make the grass grow, providing sustenance for livestock and people (vv. 7–9, 14). It is his word that causes both frost and thaw (vv. 15–18). His sustenance even extends to the ravens (v. 9), which were regarded with contempt (Leviticus 11:13–15).

God has created self-sustaining systems which govern the functioning of our planet, from the weather and oceanic currents to nutrient cycles and ecosystems. God doesn't need to operate these directly like a puppet master, yet he is always there, behind the scenes, sustaining them all. Instinctively, we inhale a blend of gases required by our body to breathe, and we consume water and food that has the nutrition required for movement. Our everyday, routine lives are totally reliant on this perfectly balanced and exquisitely designed physical world. And yet our collective actions are now changing the carefully calibrated atmosphere and degrading productive soils, increasing inequality, poverty and vulnerability.

If we believe God sustains life, what does that mean for people who love God and follow Jesus? The Israelites were encouraged to tend their farms responsibly, not harvesting the edges of the fields and allowing gleaning by the poor (Leviticus 23:22), having fallow years for the land to rest and the wild animals to eat (Leviticus 25:1–7), and keeping land in good condition for future generations. We also should live sustainably on the earth, recognising its planetary limits and not taking more than our share – we must consider what else depends on the earth for survival and flourishing. God's sustenance is not limitless; we cannot greedily draw down on nature's bounty without causing injustice to someone or something, now or in the future.

Let us praise God for his sustaining role in creation and pray for wisdom to live sustainably in this precious world we call home. Let us become active participants in God's sustenance for people and planet.

Creator God, thank you for nourishing life and sustaining earth's systems. Equip us to partner with you in caring for this delicate and diverse planet.

Hannah Gray, Programme Manager, Water Resources East

49
HOPE FOR TODAY

READ 1 CORINTHIANS 1:18–31 (NRSV)

> *Where is the one who is wise? Where is the scholar? Where is the debater of this age? Has not God made foolish the wisdom of the world? For since, in the wisdom of God, the world did not know God through wisdom, God decided, through the foolishness of the proclamation, to save those who believe. For Jews ask for signs and Greeks desire wisdom, but we proclaim Christ crucified, a stumbling block to Jews and foolishness to gentiles, but to those who are the called, both Jews and Greeks, Christ the power of God and the wisdom of God. For God's foolishness is wiser than human wisdom, and God's weakness is stronger than human strength.*

vv. 20–25

Back in the first decades after Jesus' time on earth, human-caused environmental catastrophe was still a long way over the horizon. But this extract from Paul's letter to the church in Corinth points to the same bedrock of hope on which we can stand today, because the pertinent question remains: who is the Saviour? We are all perishing: who can save us?

The Corinthian church was rather enamoured of the concept of *Sophia*, wisdom. By referring to 'wisdom' or 'the wise' 13 times in these few lines, Paul is definitely making a point! Their fixation was influenced by two religious influences in Corinth: Isis, described by Plutarch as 'a goddess exceptionally wise and a lover of wisdom', and the cult of Mithras, known for its mysterious initiation tests and multilevelled holiness. The problem was that seeking this kind of wisdom inevitably led to pride and the dangerous idea that you could, by your own wisdom, save yourself.

The dominant narrative around biodiversity loss and climate change in the UK today is that, yes, the outlook is bleak, but we will save the planet by inventing new technologies, changing our lifestyles and adapting to new conditions. While on the face of things this seems an optimistic and empowering stance, it gives us a crushing weight of responsibility. If the world's problems seem overwhelming, that is because they are if you are a human.

Paul can be harsh when the occasion calls for it. Here, he sharpens his needle and goes about bursting the Corinthians' bubble. By human standards they are rather foolish, he says. Remember that most of you have no social status or influence. You are weak, lowly and despised (vv. 26–28). And doesn't that sound like most church congregations all these centuries later?

But in the gloriously upside-down kingdom of God, these are the very people best placed to demonstrate the power, strength and wisdom of Jesus Christ. Paul's timely word for us today is that it is not on us to save the world. We can and must do all we can to serve, protect and restore the earth. But the world has a Saviour, who created it, sustains it and has pledged eternal fidelity to it.

Taking positive action demonstrates hope. It says loud and clear that we believe salvation is not only possible, but that it is also the outcome we expect and that with God's help, it will come to pass.

Creator God, thank you for keeping faith with all you have made. Give us hope in your love as we work alongside you, caring for your world. Amen.

Jo Swinney, Director of Communications, A Rocha International

50
HOPE FOR THE FUTURE

READ ROMANS 8:18–25 (NRSV)

> *I consider that the sufferings of this present time are not worth comparing with the glory about to be revealed to us. For the creation waits with eager longing for the revealing of the children of God, for the creation was subjected to futility, not of its own will, but by the will of the one who subjected it, in hope that the creation itself will be set free from its enslavement to decay and will obtain the freedom of the glory of the children of God… For in hope we were saved. Now hope that is seen is not hope, for who hopes for what one already sees? But if we hope for what we do not see, we wait for it with patience.*

vv. 18–21, 24–25

The idea that the creation, meaning here the natural world apart from humans, was 'subjected to futility' would seem at first impression to take us back to the story of Adam and Eve in the garden (Genesis 3). As a result of their sin the ground is cursed and brings up thorns and thistles, the pangs of childbirth are increased, and the husband rules the wife. We know that there has been no sudden change in the laws of nature in the 4.5 billion years of the earth's history, so it seems to me better to interpret this as the way humans in general relate to nature in the light of our sin. The Hebrew word *adam* means 'man', so Adam in the story may be taken symbolically to mean 'Everyman'.

Human sin corrupts all our relationships: first and foremost our relationship with God, then with each other and with the natural world. Today's passage relates strongly to the 'Isaiah apocalypse' of Isaiah 24—27, where we read that God is about to lay waste the earth. The earth lies polluted because its inhabitants have 'broken the everlasting covenant', and so 'a curse devours the earth' (Isaiah 24:5–6).

The good news is that this is not the end of the story. There is 'sure and certain hope', as we say at funeral services. In Isaiah 25 we read that God will 'swallow up death forever' and 'wipe away tears from all faces' (v. 8). Today's passage is similar. Both we and creation with its labour pains are groaning as we await 'the redemption of our bodies' (v. 23). What we look forward to is our own resurrection and the renewal of the whole created physical world.

We live in the 'now and not yet'. We are redeemed but await the redemption of our bodies. As Dietrich Bonhoeffer observed, our resurrection hope does not detach us from the world; it drives us back into it. We spread the good news of relationship with God restored through Christ to those who don't know it. We must also treat the natural world as we should. Evidence of the effect of human sin on creation is more evident now that at any time in human history. May our hope for the future drive us to action now to save the climate and protect threatened species.

Inspire us, Father, to love and care for our fellow humans and all your creation, as we await our co-redemption in Christ. Amen.

Rodney Holder, Astrophysicist and Priest

51
RELEASE FROM ECO-ANXIETY

READ PSALM 139 (NRSV)

> *O Lord, you have searched me and known me. You know when I sit down and when I rise up; you discern my thoughts from far away. You search out my path and my lying down and are acquainted with all my ways. Even before a word is on my tongue, O Lord, you know it completely. You hem me in, behind and before, and lay your hand upon me. Such knowledge is too wonderful for me; it is so high that I cannot attain it... Search me, O God, and know my heart; test me and know my thoughts. See if there is any wicked way in me, and lead me in the way everlasting.*

vv. 1–6, 23–24

A legitimate response to the climate crisis is anxiety. We can feel guilt for having been an active participant in a society which has caused so much damage, worry for future generations for the world they will inherit or grief for the loss of species which are no longer able to reveal our creator. Climate anxiety, which the American Psychological Association in 2017 defined as 'a chronic fear of environmental doom', is experienced within our churches as well as general society.

Climate grief encompasses the range of emotions we experience as we face any major loss: denial, anger, bargaining and depression. Sometimes these emotions hit us hard when we experience the loss of an endangered or extinct species: we grieve the disappearance of a unique expression of creation. Sometimes grief can be a gradual process, akin to watching a loved relative suffer with dementia, and we grieve for each step away from the world we knew. It's a painful process to constantly readjust to life in a new norm.

The psalmist reminds us that God knows us and is familiar with all our ways: made in his image, we feel the pain he feels as he looks at his broken world. We are created to experience his heart of justice and it is right that we are affected when we see what is happening around us. The psalm legitimises the expression of anger, frustration and anxiety to God (vv. 19–23) and joins us in calling for God's justice.

God does not leave us in a place of anxiety, worry, guilt or grief but leads us forwards into his plans (v. 16). As we allow God to search us and test our anxiety (v. 23), those emotions which are unhealthy, and which hinder us, are transformed by our creator's everlasting plans (v. 24).

The all-encompassing presence of God, which is before, behind and above us (v. 5), longs to share his precious thoughts with us: we are encouraged to listen to his voice in the midst of the anxiety and worry (v. 17). We are not meant to carry the pains and the sorrows of the world – Jesus has already done that – but we are reconciled with God to reclaim the creation mandate: to enable all of creation to flourish. With this deep knowledge of God's love for us, we can walk out of our darkness into his light, bringing him our anxiety and allowing him to lead us (v. 24).

Creator God, thank you for giving us your heart which feels pain and recognises injustice. Help us to lay our worries at your feet and work with you to bring your light into the world. Amen.

Anne Scott, Lay Church-Planting Pioneer and Outdoor Worship Network Leader

52
FREEDOM TO LIVE

READ ROMANS 6 (NRSV)

> *If we have been united with him in a death like his, we will certainly be united with him in a resurrection like his. We know that our old self was crucified with him so that the body of sin might be destroyed, so we might no longer be enslaved to sin. For whoever has died is freed from sin. But if we died with Christ, we believe that we will also live with him… Thanks be to God that you who were slaves of sin have become obedient from the heart to the form of teaching to which you were entrusted and that you, having been set free from sin, have become enslaved to righteousness… Now that you have been freed from sin and enslaved to God, the fruit you have leads to sanctification, and the end is eternal life. For the wages of sin is death, but the free gift of God is eternal life in Christ Jesus our Lord.*

vv. 5–8, 17–18, 22–23

This passage is about the sanctification of the believer in Christ. In that sense, Paul is trying to explain to the Christians in Rome the importance of living a holy life separated from sin, but it also has important implications for our relationship with creation.

Paul explains that our union with Christ in his death and resurrection means that our old sinful nature has been crucified with him. We are no longer bound to remain slaves to sin, but are now free to live a righteous life pleasing to God.

This freedom applies not only to our relationship with God, but also with creation. As Christians, we must be aware of our responsibility to care for the earth and all the creatures that inhabit it. This means that our sanctified life can have a positive impact not only on our own life, but also on creation. If we live a righteous life and respect nature, we can help to heal the damage that humanity has caused to the environment.

However, Paul also recognises that sanctification is not something that happens automatically once someone is converted in faith. Instead, it is an ongoing process that requires the believer to submit daily to the Holy Spirit and renounce his or her old sinful nature. This may include renouncing practices that harm the environment, such as excessive energy use and irresponsible exploitation of natural resources, among others. We can seek the Spirit's guidance on how we can be more aware of our ecological footprint and how we can be better stewards of our God-given creation.

Finally, the passage speaks of the ultimate reward of living a sanctified life: eternal life. But this reward applies not only to our life after death, but also to our life here. If we live a righteous life and respect God's creation, we can experience the reward of a healthier and more sustainable life on earth. Therefore, we should renounce excessive consumption of plastic, support environmental movements in their struggles and balance our diets, among other measures. If we do so, we can experience the reward of a healthier and more sustainable life on earth, because we will be generating a community spirit among God's creatures, as it was in the beginning.

God of life, I implore you that your people may become aware of the socio-environmental impact we are experiencing, that they may organise themselves and take real action in the face of it. Amen.

Steve W. Privat-Perez, Coordinator, Que Agro Con Mi Vida, and Climate Justice Activist

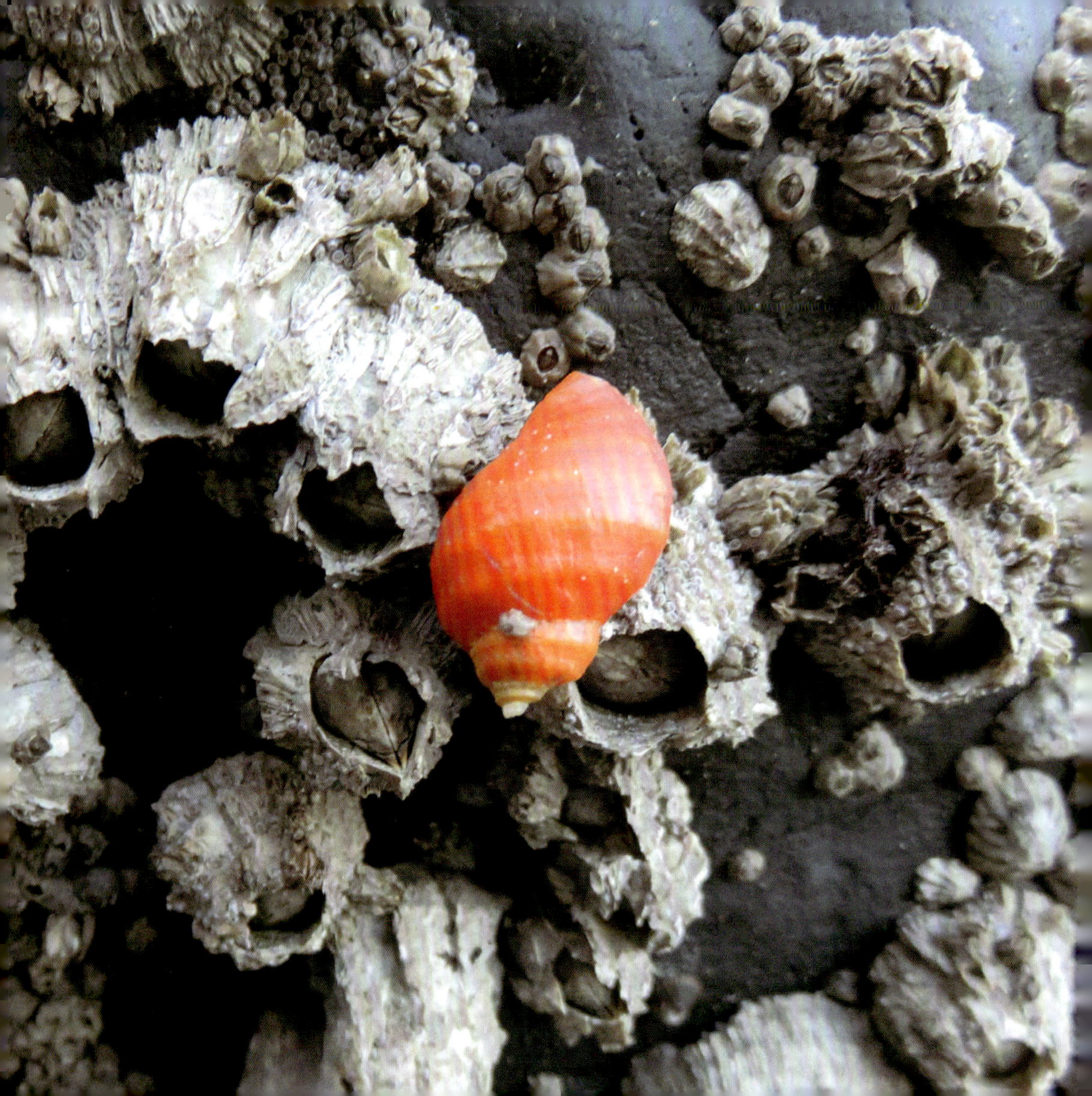

INDEX OF REFLECTIONS BY CONTRIBUTOR

Roger Abbott 130	Hannah Gray.................................. 139
Denis Alexander 15, 64	Dave Gregory 26, 39
Ruth M. Bancewicz 36, 69	Margot Hodson 133
Dave Bookless 121	Martin Hodson 137
Jennifer Brown 50	Rodney Holder 58, 72, 145
Mike Brownnutt 114	Cherryl Hunt 13
John Bryant 77	Jasmine Kwong 45
Graham Budd 116	Murdo Macdonald 74, 110
Tim Bull 93	Charmaine Mhlanga 106
Paul Ewart 23	Nathan Mladin 95
Keith Fox 32, 80	Ian Morrison 102
Davinder Gardner 55	Andrew Perrett 83
Gordon Giles 99	Sarah Perrett 60
Chris Goswami 89	Wilson Poon 21

Opposite: seashore, Vancouver Island, BC, Canada

Steve W. Privat-Perez 151	Gillian Straine 34
Vinoth Ramachandra 127	Jo Swinney 142
Rachel Siow Robertson 91	Justin Tomkins 108
Peter Robinson 112	Rebecca S. Watson 19
Hugh Rollinson 30, 52	Robert White 17, 124
Anne Scott 148	Adriel Wong 62
Patricia Shaw 97	John Wyatt 104
Meric Srokosz 48	

ACKNOWLEDGEMENTS

Many thanks to the *New Daylight* and *Guidelines* editors who originally commissioned these reflections: Sally Welch, Helen Paynter, Rachel Tranter, Olivia Warburton and Gordon Giles. Thank you also to Rachel Tranter, Olivia Warburton, Felicity Howlett, Daniele Och and the whole team at BRF Ministries for making this book a reality and getting it into people's hands.

Thank you to all the team at The Faraday Institute for Science and Religion, who supported this work from start to finish, and will continue to help launch it into the world.

This work was funded by grants from the John Templeton Foundation, Sir Halley Stewart Trust and Hinchley Charitable Trust, as well as a number of churches and individual donors.

PHOTO CREDITS

Cover and pp. 28, 136, 154 Photos © Ruth M. Bancewicz.

p. 10 A Wolf-Rayet star, by James Webb space telescope © NASA, ESA, CSA, STScI, Webb ERO Production Team on Flickr licensed under CC BY 2.0.

p. 42 Photo © Emily Hutchison.

p. 57 Osteoblasts © Kevin Mackenzie, University of Aberdeen. Source: Wellcome Collection licensed under CC BY 4.0 / cropped.

p. 66 Newly fertilised human egg. Alan Handyside. Source: Wellcome Collection. Public domain.

p. 86 AI-generated image by Ruth M. Bancewicz, created using nightcafé studio 2024.

p. 101 Neurons in the brain © Dr Jonathan Clarke. Source: Wellcome Collection licensed under CC BY 4.0 / cropped.

p. 118 Photo © Cara Parrett.

Photos of leaf shoots (pp. 9, 12, 25, etc.) by sangsiripech, stock.adobe.com

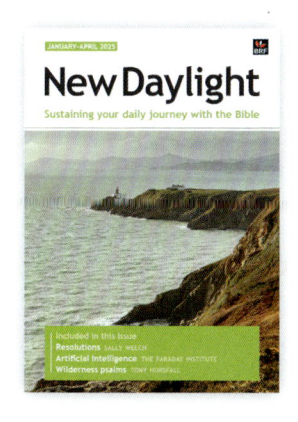

New Daylight is ideal for anyone wanting an accessible yet stimulating aid to spending time with God each day. Each issue provides four months of daily Bible readings and comment, with a team of contributors drawn from a range of church backgrounds and covering a varied selection of Old and New Testament, biblical themes, characters and seasonal readings. Edited by Gordon Giles

brfonline.org.uk/new-daylight

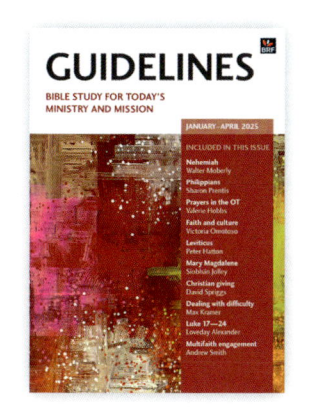

Guidelines is a unique Bible reading resource that offers four months of in-depth study, drawing on the insights of current scholarship. Its intention is to enable all its readers to interpret and apply the biblical text with confidence in today's world, while helping to equip church leaders as they meet the challenges of mission and disciple-building.
Edited by Rachel Tranter and Olivia Warburton

brfonline.org.uk/guidelines

BRF Ministries

Inspiring people of all ages to grow in Christian faith

BRF Ministries is the home of Anna Chaplaincy, Living Faith, Messy Church and Parenting for Faith

As a charity, our work would not be possible without fundraising and gifts in wills. To find out more and to donate, visit brf.org.uk/give or call +44 (0)1235 462305

Registered with FUNDRAISING REGULATOR